Chef Kathleen's
Cooking Thin Daybook

A

52-Week Plan

to

Lose Weight,

Get Fit,

and

Eat Right

CHEF KATHLEEN'S

Cooking Thin Daybook

Kathleen Daelemans

Houghton Mifflin Company   Boston   New York   2006

Copyright © 2006 by Kathleen Daelemans

For information about permission to reproduce selections from this book, write to Permissions, Houghton Mifflin Company, 215 Park Avenue South, New York, New York 10003.

Visit our Web site: www.houghtonmifflinbooks.com.

Library of Congress Cataloging-in-Publication Data
Daelemans, Kathleen.
    Chef Kathleen's cooking thin daybook : a 52-week plan to lose weight, get fit, and eat right / Kathleen Daelemans.
        p.   cm.
    ISBN-13: 978-0-618-42800-7
    ISBN-10: 0-618-42800-3
    1. Reducing diets—Recipes. 2. Weight loss. 3. Nutrition.
I. Title: Cooking thin daybook. II. Title.
    RM222.2D254 2006
    641.5'635—dc22   2005027772

Printed in the United States of America

Book design by Melissa Lotfy, adapted from Richard Oriolo's design for *Cooking Thin with Chef Kathleen*

QWT 10 9 8 7 6 5 4 3 2 1

This book is not intended to replace medical advice or be a sub-stitute for medical or other professional assistance. If you are sick or suspect that you are sick, you should see a physician. If you are taking a prescription medication, consult your physician before making changes to your diet.

    The author and the publisher expressly disclaim any respon-sibility for any adverse effects rising directly or indirectly from this book.

Acknowledgments

I WON'T GUSH, BUT THAT DOESN'T MEAN MY HEART ISN'T
filled with deep gratitude for every single person who has invested knowledge, patience, encouragement, and support in this project. Thank you, Mom and Dad, Paul, Carol, Talitha, Renie, Marc, Emily, Erin, Maya, and Douglas Anthony Williams. Thank you, Doe Coover and Rux Martin, for the years of lessons and the opportunity to learn from the best. Thank you, Frances Kennedy, Deb DeLosa, Kate Fox, Colleen Murphy, Maire Gorman, Mimi Assad, Liz Duvall, and all the behind-the-scenes talent at Houghton Mifflin.

Thank you, Miho Mizuno, for sharing your recipe for courage. Ingredients: bare-naked honesty, dignity, laughter, and a sense of mischief. Mix until pain subsides and hope springs. Dish up without delay. Repeat.

Thank you, Michael Perlman, Rainy Farrell, Maureen Petrosky, Iri Greco, Kate Lawson, Marcy Hayes, Patty Mills, Judy Debolt, and Rita Holt.

Finally, without the give-and-take exchanges that take place daily on the forums at chefkathleen.com, this book never would have come to be. As we cheer one another on, lift one another up, and share our truths, we're able to grow individually and as a community and achieve our full potential. I'm humbled by all you've taught me and all you share.

THE RECIPES Main Dishes

Soups

Roasted Squash and Onion Soup with
Cilantro ■ Week 2

Tomato, Spinach, and Tortellini Soup
■ Week 49

Potato Seafood Chowder ■ Week 17

Bacon and White Bean Soup ■ Week 7

Salads

Celery and Blue Cheese Salad ■ Week 50

Creamy Buttermilk Coleslaw ■ Week 14

Carrot Slaw ■ Week 48

Warm Wild Rice Salad with Blue Cheese,
Pears, Apples, and Toasted Walnuts
■ Week 45

Roasted Sweet Potato and Beet Salad
in Creamy Buttermilk Dressing
■ Week 11

Spinach, Cucumber, and Chickpea
Salad ■ Week 3

Chickpea, Cucumber, and Apple Salad
■ Week 20

CHICKEN

Spicy Chicken Meatballs ■ Week 18

Chicken and Wild Rice One-Pan
Supper ■ Week 21

Chicken Mushroom Stir-Fry ■ Week 28

Pan-Fried Stuffed Chicken with
Prosciutto, Mozzarella, and Basil
■ Week 26

Creamy Asian Chicken Salad ■ Week 39

Chicken and Crunchy Potato Salad
■ Week 41

FISH AND SEAFOOD

Salmon Salad with Tarragon Dressing
■ Week 5

Broiled Fish with Lemony Cucumber
Yogurt Sauce ■ Week 37

Corn, Tomato, and Shrimp Salad
■ Week 47

Hoisin Ginger Shrimp over Brown Rice
■ Week 24

BEEF AND PORK

Thai Beef Salad ■ Week 13

Grilled Beef and Chopped Vegetable
Salad ■ Week 19

Meaty Bean Fry-Pan Supper ■ Week 36

Pork Chops and Citrus Rice with
Prunes and Apricots ■ Week 22

Sausage, Chickpea, and Sweet
Potato Stew ■ Week 34

VEGETARIAN, PASTA, PIZZA, AND EGG DISHES

Mushroom Rice Stew ■ Week 9

Pasta with Roasted Fennel, Onion, and Tomatoes with Parmesan ■ Week 15

Pasta with Sweet and Hot Peppers ■ Week 46

Gourmet Asparagus, Prosciutto, and Provolone Pizza ■ Week 25

Mostly Whole-Wheat Pizza Dough ■ Week 23

Spinach, Ham, and Cheddar Pancakes ■ Week 12

Commuter Supper: Summer Squash, Basil, and Parmesan Frittata ■ Week 44

Pesto Primavera Microwave Frittata ■ Week 32

Sunday Supper for One ■ Week 35

Side Dishes

Pan-Fried Eggplant with Cilantro and Lime ■ Week 10

Eggplant with Ginger, Garlic, and Soy ■ Week 42

Sea Salt–Baked French Fries ■ Week 16

Black Bean, Corn, Tomato, and Avocado Salsa ■ Week 43

Buttermilk Zucchini Corn Muffins with Cheddar and Herbs ■ Week 33

Snacks

Better-Than-Boring Microwave Popcorn ■ Week 6

Spicy Oven-Roasted Chickpeas ■ Week 40

Binge Pickles ■ Week 30

Desserts

Peanut Butter Truffles ■ Week 1

Chocolate Fondue Party ■ Week 52

Date Orange Biscotti ■ Week 4

Nectarine and Peach Batter Cobbler ■ Week 29

Individual Upside-Down Plum Cakes ■ Week 38

Summer Berry Whips ■ Week 27

Strawberry Rhubarb Sauce ■ Week 51

Guilt-Free Vanilla Gelato ■ Week 31

Mango Shaved Ice ■ Week 8

Sharing a meal with family and friends is our opportunity to control our quality of life and our health in a time when we have so little control over anything else. Foods prepared in the true spirit of their tradition — meals meant to nurture, restore, and energize — are our connection to home, to the familiar, and to a meaningful and spiritually fulfilling future. Imparting this sense of family and caring to our children is perhaps the greatest gift we have to offer.

Whether you're on track or just beginning, it's time to assess your eating and exercise habits and state your goals. If you don't formulate a plan you can live with, Monday slips can lead to Friday hips. Instead of boo-hooing and quitting when you blow it, change your mindset. "Blowing it" isn't possible, because this isn't a diet. You're making a commitment to create an eating and exercise plan you can stick with for life. Paydays take focus and follow-through to generate, but the rewards of improved health and a body you can be proud of are among the greatest gifts you can offer to those you love.

kd@chefkathleen.com

SUBJECT: I'M SICK OF FAILING AT DIETING!

FROM: Doreen

TO: kd@chefkathleen.com

Dear Kathleen,
I go on diets and fail. I do everything perfectly, and then I really blow it. I get mad at myself and quit. How can I stop this cycle and lose the weight I want?

Doreen

REPLY: SET REALISTIC GOALS

Dear Doreen,
Give yourself permission to modify your goals and your approach as often as you see fit. If your goal is to exercise five days a week and you get in only two workouts, back up. Work toward *your* ideal, not someone else's. For instance: Ideally, I would like to achieve X by tomorrow. Realistically, I think I can do Y. And off you go. The road to ideal behavior and realized goals is paved in realistic choices. You can do this, Doreen!

Kathleen

FOOD This isn't about what you can't eat. **It's about what you *can* eat!** Most people don't meet daily quotas of good-for-you foods. Think beautiful berries, juicy, ripe tropical fruits, pears in season, the first crisp apples of fall, golden roasted squash rings on a cold winter's night, a caramely onion-topped pizza, the first sweet corn of summer, and buttermilk mashed sweet potatoes. Travel through a healthy cookbook this week and tab all the recipes that sound great.

FUN Just starting out usually means you have to cut back on calories, which for me feels like someone's ripping the baby from my arms. Filling this void is key. **A pot of warm tea with milk and honey is a soothing way to stave off false hunger pangs and tide you over till mealtime.** Splurge on a selection of teas you've always wanted to try, a beautiful jar of honey you "can't afford," and a one-of-a-kind perfect teacup to drink it from.

FITNESS Drag out your fitness wardrobe. If your gym shoes second as lawnmowing shoes and tromp-through-puddles-to-grab-the-paper shoes, consider buying a new pair. **If you hate the way you feel in your exercise clothes, do something about it.** Mix and match what you have until you come up with at least one outfit that makes you feel confident. If you have "nothing to wear," go shopping already!

FOCUS Make up your mind that you're going to succeed at this weight game once and for all. You heard me. **Decide that you can do this, and you will.** Attitude drives behavior.

Homework Assignment

Homework Assignment Make a list of eating habits you'd like to change. For each "bad" habit, write down what your ideal self would consume. Although some people can cold-turkey their way out of Big Mac land, I cannot. For those of you who can't either, next to each bad habit, write down a better habit.

Bad habit *I eat too many burger meals every week.*

Better habit *I'll cut out one burger meal a week and order the kid size next time.*

Ideal habit *When I want burgers and fries, I'll make my own, using lean ground beef or chicken. I'll portion-control the patties and serve them on whole-grain buns with baked sweet potato fries.*

YOUR GAME PLAN (STATE YOUR FOOD AND EXERCISE GOALS FOR THE WEEK)

Peanut Butter Truffles

MAKES 16 TRUFFLES *You didn't think this was going to be an awful diet book without any treats, did you? When you're going through vending-machine withdrawal, these nutrient-rich peanut butter truffles really hit the spot. Make yourself dig out the food processor: the truffles will mix better. Crunchy peanut butter is drier than creamy, so if you use it, you may need an extra drizzle of honey to bind them.*

½ **cup creamy peanut butter**
½ **cup nonfat dry milk powder**
¼ **cup wheat germ**
¼ **cup old-fashioned oatmeal**
2–3 **teaspoons honey**

COMBINE all ingredients in a food processor and pulse or mix until thoroughly combined.

ROLL into a rope and cut 16 equal slices. Roll each slice into a round ball and serve. So you're not tempted to eat too many, wrap them individually. They will keep for 1 week refrigerated and up to a month frozen.

GO NUTS!

Harvard School of Public Health researchers report that consuming 1 tablespoon of peanut butter five or more times per week can help you reduce your risk of developing type 2 diabetes by 20 percent. Consume an ounce of peanuts or other nuts instead, and you can reduce your risk by 30 percent.

But all peanut butters aren't created equal. Compare labels with an eye for calorie, fat, and sugar quantities. Every little calorie savings helps. Measure out a single serving, 2 *level* tablespoons, so you know what it looks like. You heard me; get out the measuring spoons and get busy.

Monday

What I ate:

What I wish I hadn't:

What I did for exercise:

Tuesday

What I ate:

What I wish I hadn't:

What I did for exercise:

Wednesday

What I ate:

What I wish I hadn't:

What I did for exercise:

Thursday

What I ate:

What I wish I hadn't:

What I did for exercise:

Friday

What I ate:

What I wish I hadn't:

What I did for exercise:

REPORT CARD

I REALLY FELT GREAT WHEN I

I CAN GET BETTER AT

NEW FOODS I'M GOING TO TRY

NEXT WEEK I'M GOING TO

GIVE YOURSELF A GRADE
FOR THIS WEEK'S EFFORTS:

Saturday

What I ate:

What I wish I hadn't:

What I did for exercise:

Sunday

What I ate:

What I wish I hadn't:

What I did for exercise:

No matter what you're doing for fitness, think quality over speed, quantity over inaction, variety over complacency. Boredom is your cue to change. Lethargy is your cue to kick into high gear. When you think you can't take another step, remember that the keys to change are in your hand. Choose to "have no time" or choose to make eating right and exercising a priority. Choose to make every exercise minute count or choose to count the minutes. Choose to make your calories work for you or choose to let them fill out your fat clothes. Choices dictate outcome. Choose change and you will.

kd@chefkathleen.com

SUBJECT: GUNG-HO — FOR THE FIRST WEEK

FROM: Gabby

TO: kd@chefkathleen.com

Dear Kathleen,
I've gained about twenty-five pounds since high school. I enjoy eating out with friends and trying new restaurants. I think I've purchased about five gym memberships over the past five years. I'm all gung-ho the first week, and then I quit. How have you been able to stay consistent all these years?

Gabby

REPLY: LESS ISN'T MORE

Dear Gabby,
I live to eat. If I don't exercise, I can't eat the foods I love in the quantities I want. A half-cup serving of ice cream is a little too small for me, and two warm homemade cookies are at least one shy of satisfying. I *gotta* exercise. If I move less, I have to eat less. If I move more, I can eat more! When I calculated that a girl my height can burn 265 calories in an hour of walking, I was happy, but when I learned that I can burn 795 calories an hour riding my bike, I was ecstatic! I spend the better part of my rides fantasizing about the treats I'm earning.

Kathleen

FOOD **Throw together a batch of Roasted Squash and Onion Soup with Cilantro.** Serve it with warm crusty bread and a green salad with sautéed spinach or Swiss chard or microwave-steamed green beans. Of course there's no "starch." Fill up on starch and fill out your pants. Fill up on veggies and watch your pants fall to the floor.

FUN Play! **Give yourself a day off from your regular routine and go play outside.** Ride your bike, sign up for belly-dancing classes, take a surfing lesson, hike through fall foliage, or go shopping! With the right mindset, exercise can become play. According to *USA Today*, in West Virginia, where childhood obesity rates are at an all-time high, the West Virginia Public Employees Insurance Agency recruited children to participate in an at-home study using the video game Dance Dance Revolution to increase activity. Eleven-year-old K. D. Jones, who weighed 175 pounds, lost 10 pounds playing the game, and his mom, who struggles with her weight, is giving it a try too.

FITNESS Feel like a million bucks for the price of a Post-it note. **Tape this week's fitness goals to the bathroom mirror.** Tape a copy on the edge of your computer screen and another copy on your cell phone if you have to. You can try to ignore that which won't go away. Or you can read your goals and follow through. The act of reading them will give you the incentive you need to follow through.

FOCUS Consistently visualize the sense of accomplishment you'll feel when you meet your fitness goals this week. **See your improved self in your mind's eye.** Think about how much more in control you'll feel. That's how you're going to make it.

Homework Assignment
Challenge yourself to increase the quality, quantity, and variety of exercise you're doing this week. Write down at least one thing in each category you know you can achieve by Friday.

Quality *If walking is your exercise of choice, can you improve your posture? Can you concentrate on swinging your arms with each step?*

Quantity *Can you increase the number of minutes you swing your arms? Can you increase the number of minutes you walk each day? Can you increase the number of times you walk this week by one walk or more?*

Variety *Can you drive to a nearby park or beach and walk there? Can you do your route in reverse? Can you invent a new route this week?*

YOUR GAME PLAN (STATE YOUR FOOD AND EXERCISE GOALS FOR THE WEEK)

Roasted Squash and Onion Soup with Cilantro

SERVES 4 TO 6 *If you've never cooked with winter squash, this recipe is the perfect excuse to start. Any variety will do. A pinch of cinnamon added to the soup just before serving complements the caramely roasted flavors of the squash and onions. The cilantro adds a gorgeous brightness. Serve with a hunk of warm whole-grain bread and a simple garden-lettuce salad.*

1 medium winter squash, such as butternut, acorn, or hubbard (about 2 pounds), peeled, cut in half, and seeded

1 large onion, cut into 4 wedges
Olive oil for brushing

2 cups chicken broth

1 teaspoon ground cinnamon

1/2 cup loosely packed, coarsely chopped fresh cilantro

PREHEAT oven to 425°F. Brush surfaces of squash and onion with olive oil. Place on cookie sheet and cook for 35 to 45 minutes, or until squash is cooked through and tender to the touch. Cool slightly.

SCRAPE squash meat into a large soup pot. Chop onion and add to pot. Add chicken broth and 2 cups water and bring to a boil. Reduce heat to a simmer, add cinnamon, and cook for 1 to 2 minutes, or until very hot. Turn off heat, add cilantro, and stir. Serve.

Monday

What I ate:

What I wish I hadn't:

What I did for exercise:

Tuesday

What I ate:

What I wish I hadn't:

What I did for exercise:

WEEK
2

Wednesday

What I ate:

What I wish I hadn't:

What I did for exercise:

Thursday

What I ate:

What I wish I hadn't:

What I did for exercise:

Friday

What I ate:

What I wish I hadn't:

What I did for exercise:

REPORT CARD

I REALLY FELT GREAT WHEN I

I CAN GET BETTER AT

NEW FOODS I'M GOING TO TRY

NEXT WEEK I'M GOING TO

GIVE YOURSELF A GRADE
FOR THIS WEEK'S EFFORTS:

What I ate:

What I wish I hadn't:

What I did for exercise:

Sunday

What I ate:

What I wish I hadn't:

What I did for exercise:

Turn shame into good gains. The only way to get out from underneath the guilt and shame of lousy habits is to overcome them. You're not a helpless victim. Review and reassess your goals and get busy!

Zero in on your absolute worst habit and tackle that baby. Get rid of binge foods, seek outside support in the form of counseling if that's what it takes, and create healthy outlets. Finger paints aren't just for preschoolers, you know. Art therapy is good, clean fun. Read books, garden, collect something, babysit small children—anything to take your mind off your troubles and heal your soul.

kd@chefkathleen.com

SUBJECT: BUMMED OUT
FROM: Rachel
TO: kd@chefkathleen.com

Dear Kathleen,
I'm really embarrassed about my weight. I make bad choices. I know what I need to do, but I feel like such a loser. How did you get past this?
Rachel

REPLY: GET OVER IT!

Dear Rachel,
I get past it by maintaining an honest dialogue with myself and by accessing support and creating accountability when I need it. If I consume too many calories, no matter how tired or unmotivated I'm feeling, I don't ignore the exercise nag that pops into my head. I call or e-mail a friend or post a note on the forums at chefkathleen.com to say I'm on my way out the door for a walk or a bike ride. Telling someone creates forward motion and an expectation that I need to follow through because someone might ask how my workout went. There's nothing worse than having to say I didn't go.
Kathleen

FOOD **Cut back, cut out, trade up!** Choose one food item you need to cut back on and, starting now, switch it out for something you need to work in. Cut back: If 4 o'clock M&M's are keeping you out of your skinny jeans, how about half a bag? Cut out: How about a handful of healthy trail mix with a few M&M's thrown in and a bottle of water? Trade up: How about a scrambled-egg-white sandwich with scallions, chives, and grated extra-sharp cheddar on barely toasted whole-grain bread?

FUN Heal your heart and build your self-esteem through play. **Spend an hour doing something you love to do but haven't done in a zillion years.** Buy a flat of impatiens and plant them, paint a weathered garden chair a cheery color even if it's winter, sign up for an art class, or visit a nearby gallery you've been meaning to check out for years.

FITNESS Feeling like a wildly panting dog when you're working out is enough to make anyone want to quit. **Focus on your breathing this week.** When you start to feel out of control, pull back a little, take deep breaths, and focus on your form. When you feel in control, up the intensity a little.

FOCUS Every time you look in the mirror, acknowledge your accomplishments, smile, and visualize your "after" shot. **No matter where you're at today, you have the power to be ahead of the game tomorrow.**

Homework Assignment Review your homework assignments for Weeks 1 and 2. Review the mini goals you've set. If you're on track, good for you! If you're not, identify where you're having trouble. Next to each challenge, write down why you think you didn't reach your goals. Honesty counts. Revise your ambitions by thinking realistically. For instance, if getting a fruit in at breakfast is too hard, can you work one in later in the morning? If you can't get in five work-outs a week, shoot for four.

YOUR GAME PLAN (STATE YOUR FOOD AND EXERCISE GOALS FOR THE WEEK)

Spinach, Cucumber, and Chickpea Salad

SERVES 4 TO 6 *This spinach, cucumber, and chickpea salad with a zesty, lemony cumin vinai-grette is superquick to prepare and satisfying. Oprah invited me on her show to cook for a woman with type 2 diabetes who didn't think she could eat anything that tasted good and still lose weight. We did a pizza party makeover and served this salad as the gorgeous side. She loved it.*

½ cup fresh lemon juice

¾ teaspoon ground cumin
   Coarse salt

2 tablespoons olive oil (optional)

1 pint cherry tomatoes, halved

1 English cucumber, peeled seeded, and thinly sliced

4 scallions, white parts only, thinly sliced

1 15-ounce can chickpeas, drained and rinsed

½ cup coarsely chopped fresh flat-leaf parsley

½ cup coarsely chopped fresh mint

   Half a 10-ounce bag salad greens (the healthiest kind you can stand)

   Half a 10-ounce bag prewashed baby spinach

IN the bowl you'll serve the salad in, whisk together lemon juice, cumin, salt, and olive oil. Add tomatoes, cuke, scallions, chickpeas, parsley, and mint. Toss to combine. Add salad greens and spinach. Toss, taste, adjust seasonings, and serve.

■ *If you want to up the good calories, shredded carrots and diced mango are really delicious in this salad. If you're serving it as an entrée and you've got a meat eater to satisfy, put thinly sliced grilled flank steak or chicken on top. Or keep it vegetarian and serve it over bulgur.*

Monday

What I ate:

What I wish I hadn't:

What I did for exercise:

Tuesday

What I ate:

What I wish I hadn't:

What I did for exercise:

Wednesday

What I ate:

What I wish I hadn't:

What I did for exercise:

Thursday

What I ate:

What I wish I hadn't:

What I did for exercise:

Friday

What I ate:

What I wish I hadn't:

What I did for exercise:

Saturday

I REALLY FELT GREAT WHEN I

What I ate:

What I wish I hadn't:

I CAN GET BETTER AT

What I did for exercise:

Sunday

NEW FOODS I'M GOING TO TRY

What I ate:

What I wish I hadn't:

NEXT WEEK I'M GOING TO

What I did for exercise:

GIVE YOURSELF A GRADE FOR THIS WEEK'S EFFORTS:

Will yourself to want to change. It's easy to declare that you want to change your ways, but if there's no heartfelt desire behind the statement, you'll stay rooted in the space you're occupying.

Hang up the Do Not Disturb sign and call up that grain of hope that bubbles to the surface on days you're feeling good. Write down all of your hopes, dreams, and wishes. Write down why you want each and every item on your list. Write down your rock-bottom deadline for achieving each of them. Passion ignites action. Action *is* change. All your dreams *can* come true, you know.

kd@chefkathleen.com

SUBJECT: PENNY WISE, POUND FOOLISH

FROM: Gael

TO: kd@chefkathleen.com

Dear Kathleen,
Our budget is very tight, so I can't afford to spend extra money on a health club membership. I have a five- and seven-year-old that keep me superbusy. What can I do at home that will help me lose the 50 pounds I've gained since college?

Gael

REPLY: LAUNCH YOUR HOME HEALTH CLUB

Dear Gael,
Is there a time of day you can put the kids in a little wagon and take walks together? I realize this won't be "fun" five days a week, but perhaps two days of walking with the kids combined with three days of working out to exercise videos or DVDs would work. You can choose from a variety of different workouts: weight training, aerobics, dancing, yoga, Pilates, and more. There are programs for all fitness levels, and you can do them when it's convenient for you. My advice is to design your game plan and a strict, nonnegotiable schedule to go with it.

Kathleen

FOOD Do, or dine on donuts? The best-laid plans seem to run amuck when you have the least amount of energy. **Write down anything you can think of that might get in the way of healthy meals this week.** Write down three instant-gratification dinners you can get on the table faster than you can fall off the wagon. Do this now and when you get into a do-or-dine-on-donuts moment, you'll have everything in place to make the right choices. Canned refried beans, scrambled egg whites, and salsa on a warm whole-wheat tortilla is better for you than carryout any day.

FUN Take a time-out and watch a daytime cooking show for a little culinary inspiration. **If the recipes you see are too "chubby," challenge yourself to come up with ways to slim them down.** Up the veggies and cut the sugar and fats by 25 percent, and no one will notice. Post the recipe on the forums at chefkathleen.com, and I'll slim it down for you.

FITNESS Does your exercise routine support achieving rock-hard results? **Wanting to get in shape will never happen if your intentions don't drive your actions.** Give 50 percent, and you'll get 50 percent. Give 100 percent, and you'll earn 100 percent. Don't waste your time. Don't start late, don't leave early. Don't watch the clock. Embrace the time you've set aside to work out. Give it everything that you have in you, and walk away proud.

FOCUS Dream. Think about where you want to be in one year, next month, and tomorrow. Visualize yourself in each scenario right down to the outfit you'll be wearing at the finish line. **See and believe, and you will become.** Practice visualization every chance you get.

Homework Assignment

Recap! Write down every new eating and exercise behavior you've turned into a habit. Acknowledge your accomplishments. Tell someone! Next to each accomplishment, write down how you can take yourself to the next level in that area. If you've mastered salads at lunch but are still falling short in the fruit and veggie department each day, write down a way you think you can work in more of what you're missing. If you're walking but you're not feeling or seeing results, are you ready to do something else? Can you try to work in one minute of jogging for every five minutes of walking?

YOUR GAME PLAN (STATE YOUR FOOD AND EXERCISE GOALS FOR THE WEEK)

Date Orange Biscotti

MAKES 12 BARS *Whole-wheat pastry flour is easy to find in the markets and is a very simple way to up the nutrition in many baking recipes. If you don't like biscotti crisp, add another $1/4$ cup orange juice for a moister cookie.*

½ **cup whole-wheat pastry flour**
½ **cup all-purpose flour**
⅛ **teaspoon salt**
½ **teaspoon baking powder**
¼ **teaspoon baking soda**
3 **tablespoons unsalted butter, at room temperature**
⅓ **cup dark brown sugar**
1 **teaspoon finely grated orange zest**
1 **large egg**
¼ **cup orange juice**
½ **cup chopped walnuts**
1 **cup chopped pitted dates**

PREHEAT oven to 350°F. In a small bowl, sift together both flours, salt, baking powder, and baking soda.

IN a large bowl with an electric mixer on medium to high, beat butter and brown sugar until creamy. Add orange zest and egg until combined. Add orange juice, mixing until incorporated. Fold in flour mixture until just combined.

STIR in walnuts and dates. Mix until combined.

SPREAD batter in an ungreased 2-quart baking dish and bake for 25 minutes, or until a toothpick inserted into center comes out clean. Cool in pan on a wire rack, 10 to 12 minutes, or until cool enough to handle. Slice into 12 bars and reduce oven heat to 325°F. Place bars on a cookie sheet and bake for 25 minutes more, or until crisp.

Monday

What I ate:

What I wish I hadn't:

What I did for exercise:

Tuesday

What I ate:

What I wish I hadn't:

What I did for exercise:

Wednesday

What I ate:

What I wish I hadn't:

What I did for exercise:

Thursday

What I ate:

What I wish I hadn't:

What I did for exercise:

Friday

What I ate:

What I wish I hadn't:

What I did for exercise:

Saturday

I REALLY FELT GREAT WHEN I

What I ate:

I CAN GET BETTER AT

What I wish I hadn't:

What I did for exercise:

NEW FOODS I'M GOING TO TRY

Sunday

What I ate:

NEXT WEEK I'M GOING TO

What I wish I hadn't:

What I did for exercise:

GIVE YOURSELF A GRADE
FOR THIS WEEK'S EFFORTS:

My kitchen isn't big enough to throw a cat through sideways. But that doesn't matter. It's neat and tidy, and I like to cook in it. A kitchen that's set up for quick cooking isn't brain-surgery hard to organize and doesn't cost a fortune. Clean up the place and stock it like I'm coming to visit and we're going to cook the next seven suppers from scratch. Cook at home more than you eat out. You'll lose weight more quickly and maintain good health more easily. Guaranteed.

kd@chefkathleen.com

SUBJECT: DON'T MAKE ME EAT THOSE CEREALS!

FROM: Max

TO: kd@chefkathleen.com

Dear Kathleen,
My doctor wants me to lose weight and eat more fiber. I can't stand those high-fiber cereals, and I can't get my husband or kids to eat them. What other foods have fiber? And what's so great about fiber anyway?

  Max

REPLY: GET SOME MORAL FIBER

Dear Max,
Fiber helps you feel full. When I'm full, I don't overeat. When I don't overeat, I don't pack on pounds. Doctors like fiber for reasons other than whether it'll help you keep your dessert spoon out of the ice cream, and I do too. Research shows that a diet low in saturated fat and cholesterol that includes soluble fiber can help reduce risks of diabetes, some cancers, and heart disease.

  All kinds of foods have fiber. Try oatmeal, oat bran, rice bran, wheat bran, soybeans, black beans, peas, and chickpeas. And also: citrus fruits, blackberries, mangoes, strawberries, squash, sweet potatoes, artichokes, avocados, cabbage, and Brussels sprouts. Surely you like some of these?

  Kathleen

FOOD **Add another veggie to tonight's dinner.** Just for fun, make it a different color from the ones you're used to eating. Supergood-for-you, kid-friendly spaghetti squash can be on the table before everyone gets washed up for supper. With a fork, pierce squash in 7 places. Place on paper towel in microwave oven. Microwave on high for 10 to 12 minutes, turning 3 times, until squash gives slightly when pressed. Remove from oven and let stand until cool enough to handle, about 5 minutes. Cut squash in half lengthwise and, using a spoon, discard seeds. With a fork, remove flesh from shell (it will come out in spaghetti-like strands). Toss with a drizzle of olive oil or a small pat of butter and a sprinkling of Parmesan cheese. Season with salt and pepper to taste.

FUN **Draft a wish list of every pot, pan, and gadget you've always wanted to have in your kitchen.** Paste that list on the fridge. Every time you reach an eating or exercise goal, collect a new gadget or save up your gold stars and splurge on something more expensive once every few months or so. Rewards with health benefits and weight-loss payoffs are worth the price of admission.

FITNESS **Try the Clean-Your-House Diet.** Make extra trips to and from the basement when you're doing laundry, put the dishes away one at a time to add extra steps, vacuum the house twice as fast, do the windows more often. A ringing phone is your cue to grab the portable phone and move. Build more physical movement into your day, and the results will meet you in the mirror.

FOCUS **Adversity frees potential.** Chase it down.

Homework Assignment Empty your cupboards and drawers of all your pots and pans and other cooking equipment. Take a look—do you have three pots with no lids, two lids without pots, a nonstick skillet with no Teflon coating? Begin to organize your kitchen to support the way you use it. There's nothing more liberating than the feeling you get after you've organized something.

YOUR GAME PLAN (STATE YOUR FOOD AND EXERCISE GOALS FOR THE WEEK)

Salmon Salad with Tarragon Dressing

SERVES 4 *This lively little supper is perfect for entertaining. The dressing can be made the night before, and the veggies can be prepared in advance too.*

FOR THE DRESSING
MAKES ½ CUP

- ¼ cup champagne vinegar
- 2 tablespoons olive oil
- 1 teaspoon sugar
- ½ small onion, coarsely chopped
- 1 tablespoon fresh tarragon leaves
- Coarse salt and cracked black pepper

FOR THE SALAD AND SALMON

- 8 ounces celery, thinly sliced
- 1 small head fennel, cored and very thinly sliced
- 1 small carrot, peeled and very thinly sliced
- 4–5 radishes, very thinly sliced
- 2 cups washed torn salad greens, such as arugula, radicchio, or butter lettuce
- 2 teaspoons olive oil
- 1 pound salmon, cut into 4 pieces

DRESSING: Place all ingredients except salt and pepper in a blender. Blend until smooth. Season to taste with salt and pepper.

SALAD AND SALMON: Mix celery, fennel, carrot, radishes, and salad greens in a bowl. Add tarragon dressing and toss. Divide among four serving plates.

PLACE oil in a large nonstick skillet over medium-high heat. When hot but not smoking, place salmon in pan skin side up and cook on both sides until golden brown, 2 to 3 minutes per side.

PLACE salmon on top of vegetables and serve immediately.

■ *You can grill the salmon if you're not in the mood to heat up the kitchen, and you can also substitute white wine vinegar for champagne vinegar.*

Monday

What I ate:

What I wish I hadn't:

What I did for exercise:

Tuesday

What I ate:

What I wish I hadn't:

What I did for exercise:

Wednesday

What I ate:

What I wish I hadn't:

What I did for exercise:

Thursday

What I ate:

What I wish I hadn't:

What I did for exercise:

Friday

What I ate:

What I wish I hadn't:

What I did for exercise:

I REALLY FELT GREAT WHEN I

I CAN GET BETTER AT

NEW FOODS I'M GOING TO TRY

NEXT WEEK I'M GOING TO

GIVE YOURSELF A GRADE
FOR THIS WEEK'S EFFORTS:

Saturday

What I ate:

What I wish I hadn't:

What I did for exercise:

Sunday

What I ate:

What I wish I hadn't:

What I did for exercise:

WEEK 6
Beat Back the Ding Dong Demons

Hidden edible treasures will sabotage you faster than an ice cream sundae sitting in front of you. When you're home alone and the cupboards are stocked with teenage-babysitter cuisine, they'll call your name 24/7 until you've consumed every last bit. Ding Dong–proof your cupboards of foods too tempting to have around and take an armed guard with you when you shop for groceries so you don't repeat the offense of purchasing that stuff in the first place.

kd@chefkathleen.com

SUBJECT: I CAN'T EAT JUST ONE!

FROM: Marta

TO: kd@chefkathleen.com

Dear Kathleen,
When I start eating potato chips, I usually eat more than half the bag. Any suggestions?
Marta

REPLY: IT'S CRUNCH TIME

Dear Marta,
Multiple-choice answer:

1. Keep the chips in your house and let them torture you.

2. Swap full-fat chips for baked chips and portion them into small snack-size bags the day you bring them into the house.

3. Get them out of your house altogether and be done with the problem. If they're not there, they can't tempt you!

4. The next time you really get a craving for chips, walk to the store to get them.

When my nieces want ice cream, they have to ride their bikes the four-mile round trip to the Dairy Queen, which I usually stretch to six miles by enticing them to go along the waterfront so we can check out what's happening down at the lake.

Kathleen

FOOD I test good-for-me recipes almost every Thursday and make five to seven different entrées and portion them into single-size servings and freeze them. When I'm starving, I pull one out, throw it in the microwave, and it's ready to eat within five minutes. Do I love the work at the time? Not always. But I'm grateful each and every time I reach for a lifesaver meal. **This week, choose recipes that will allow you to get ahead and make a double batch of everything for the purpose of freezing it.** Double up on a recipe that serves 6 to 8. Try the Sausage, Chickpea, and Sweet Potato Stew in Week 34, and you'll have 6 to 8 meals in the freezer. Make double batches of three different meals this week, and you'll have 12 to 16 meals in the freezer!

FUN Rent a really funny movie and whip up a batch of air-popped or microwave popcorn. Not the 100-calories per serving microwave kind but the kind that starts with corn kernels. See the recipe on the next page for better-than-boring air-popped popcorn.

FITNESS Repeat after me: interval training. **When you're walking, try jogging for thirty seconds every five minutes or so.** Or if you're riding your bike, try to sprint one minute every ten minutes. These bursts of business will help you burn more calories and improve your fitness level.

FOCUS Every time the Mars bar machine beckons you, remember that regular-size candy bars contain about 250 calories. You won't burn that off walking back to your desk. An hour of power walking or two hours of vigorous housecleaning or an extra three hours at your computer desk would get the job done. **But do you really want to walk four miles or clean four zillion windows at race pace for a lousy candy bar?**

Homework Assignment

What would hidden cameras reveal in your house? What if there were cameras in your nightstand? Don't be the woman who hides candy bars in her soup pots, the teenager who keeps a stash of junk food to rival a convenience store under her bed, or the dark-chocolate pack rat. You have two choices—you can march straight to the kitchen with this book in hand and do a clean sweep of your cupboards to align your environment with your health and weight-loss goals, or you can do nothing and flounder awhile longer.

YOUR GAME PLAN (STATE YOUR FOOD AND EXERCISE GOALS FOR THE WEEK)

Better-Than-Boring Microwave Popcorn

SERVES 1

PLACE ¼ cup unpopped corn kernels in a brown paper lunch bag and staple shut. Place in microwave on high for 2 to 3 minutes, or until there are no more than 5 seconds between pops.

SHOWSTOPPING TOPPERS

freshly grated Parmigiano-Reggiano cheese

Cabot Cheese's Cheddar Shake

white cheddar popcorn seasoning (available near the spices in your grocery store)

Sarah's Sea Salt (available at Whole Foods)

any sodium-free or seasoning mix you like

■ *Think jerk chicken, taco, or Cajun spice mixes, or even dried pizza herbs.* ■ *If you're not happy with the fact that seasonings fall to the bottom of the bowl, lightly mist the popcorn with spray oil and then sprinkle on seasonings.*

10 REASONS TO LOVE HOMEMADE MICROWAVE POPCORN

Munching on popcorn at the movies can cost you a day's worth of calories and a week's worth of fat! Read on:

Serving Size	Calories	Total Fat	Saturated Fat
Kid's (5 cups)	300	20	14
Kid's with butter	470	37	22
Small (7 cups)	400	27	19
Small with butter	630	50	29
Medium (11 cups)	650	43	31
Medium with butter	910	71	41
Large (16 cups)	900	60	43
Large with butter	1220	97	56
Extra-large (20 cups)	1160	77	55
Extra-large with butter	1640	126	73

What I ate:

What I wish I hadn't:

What I did for exercise:

Tuesday

What I ate:

What I wish I hadn't:

What I did for exercise:

Wednesday

What I ate:

What I wish I hadn't:

What I did for exercise:

Thursday

What I ate:

What I wish I hadn't:

What I did for exercise:

Friday

What I ate:

What I wish I hadn't:

What I did for exercise:

REPORT CARD

I REALLY FELT GREAT WHEN I

I CAN GET BETTER AT

NEW FOODS I'M GOING TO TRY

NEXT WEEK I'M GOING TO

GIVE YOURSELF A GRADE
FOR THIS WEEK'S EFFORTS:

Saturday

What I ate:

What I wish I hadn't:

What I did for exercise:

Sunday

What I ate:

What I wish I hadn't:

What I did for exercise:

Scrutinize every single pantry item and sweep your cupboards clean of "holler" foods—the ones that call your name until you gorge on them. Rationalizing "necessary" foods because you don't want to waste the money you spent on them or because they're "just for the kids" isn't serving anyone's health needs. While mac-and-cheese meals, boxed stuffing, biscuit mix, and chicken pot pies may not be the obvious bad guys that chocolate bars, Toaster Tarts, and cheese curls are, a lot of today's "convenience foods" serve up inconvenient levels of calories, cholesterol, fat, and sodium. From here on out, every single food item purchased must serve your body and your goals. Stock your pantry to cook healthfully, and you will.

OAT CUISINE

My dad is a coffee-and-donuts kind of guy. But when his doctor laid down the law for him to lower his cholesterol or else, my mom shoved a bowl of oatmeal in front of him that very morning, and every day since. In four months he lowered his cholesterol by 30 points. He didn't always eat the oatmeal for breakfast—sometimes it was a midday snack or late-night grub. But he stuck to the plan, and now he's back in the good graces of his doctor.

FOOD Got oatmeal? Seventy percent of participants in Quaker's Heart-Smart Challenge lowered their cholesterol by 16.9 percent by eating a bowl of oatmeal every day for 30 days. **Have your cholesterol checked, take your own thirty-day challenge, and check it again.**

FUN If you've never been to a "health food store," make an expedition. **Go to your local Whole Foods type store and check out all the great funky pantry ingredients you can use to spice up your recipes and slim down your cooking.** The one near me has a spectacular seafood section, museum-quality fruits and vegetables, every whole grain you can think of and a handful you've never heard of, wonderful cheeses and nuts, lots of great spices, unusual oils and vinegars, and beautiful teas. When money's tight, wandering through the gorgeous displays is enough to recharge your enthusiasm for cooking and send you home renewed.

FITNESS Only 27 percent of American adults get enough leisure-time exercise to achieve cardiovascular fitness. **Thirty minutes a day of low to moderate activity can deliver heart health benefits.** Grooving to the oldies, swinging to FitTV or videos at home, square dancing, kayaking, mountain biking, and water aerobics are great ways to work in cardio fun.

FOCUS **Find out if you're at risk for heart disease and stroke, and research what you can do to reinvent your destiny.** Visit americanheart.org or call 1-888-4STROKE to learn all about the disease and its prevention.

Homework Assignment Stock your pantry, fridge, and freezer with heart-healthy, cholesterol-lowering foods:

* Fish, such as salmon, trout, sardines, and mackerel

* Legumes, such as dried beans or canned beans, peas, and lentils (When reaching for canned items, go for the low-sodium brands.)

* Tofu, edamame (soybean pods), soy milk, and soy burgers

* Oatmeal, which is rich in soluble fiber

* Olive oil, a monounsaturated fat

YOUR GAME PLAN (STATE YOUR FOOD AND EXERCISE GOALS FOR THE WEEK)

Bacon and White Bean Soup

SERVES 4 *A little bacon can entice even the most bean-shy diners into trying at least a few spoonfuls.*

1 teaspoon olive oil

1 ounce pancetta or country bacon, cut thick and diced

2 garlic cloves, thinly sliced lengthwise

4 sprigs fresh thyme or 1 teaspoon dried

2 15-ounce cans white beans, drained and rinsed

½ teaspoon crushed red chili flakes

3 cups chicken broth

PUT olive oil, pancetta, garlic, and thyme in a large pot. Cook over medium heat, stirring often, until garlic is golden, about 5 minutes.

ADD beans and chili flakes and stir to coat evenly. Add broth. Bring to a boil, reduce heat to strong simmer, and cook until beans are heated through, about 5 minutes. Discard thyme sprigs and serve.

■ *Add some freshly chopped spinach, baby spinach, or Swiss chard during the last few minutes of cooking.*

Monday

What I ate:

What I wish I hadn't:

What I did for exercise:

Tuesday

What I ate:

What I wish I hadn't:

What I did for exercise:

Wednesday

What I ate:

What I wish I hadn't:

What I did for exercise:

Thursday

What I ate:

What I wish I hadn't:

What I did for exercise:

Friday

What I ate:

What I wish I hadn't:

What I did for exercise:

Saturday

I REALLY FELT GREAT WHEN I

I CAN GET BETTER AT

NEW FOODS I'M GOING TO TRY

NEXT WEEK I'M GOING TO

GIVE YOURSELF A GRADE
FOR THIS WEEK'S EFFORTS:

What I ate:

What I wish I hadn't:

What I did for exercise:

Sunday

What I ate:

What I wish I hadn't:

What I did for exercise:

After seven weeks of healthier eating, more vigorous exercise, and making good but hard choices, you may be experiencing I-wanna-quit fits, fitness burnout, and food ruts. Do you want to bloat the statistic that says most people fail at dieting? Understanding the legitimate reasons you plateau is key to working through them.

kd@chefkathleen.com

SUBJECT: MOODY BLUES
FROM: BethAnne
TO: kd@chefkathleen.com

Dear Kathleen,
I'm really down. I know I should keep at this, but it's too hard.
*   BethAnne*

REPLY: DON'T GO IT ALONE

Dear BethAnne,
When you're really feeling down, the challenge is to get yourself out of bed or at least to the computer, where you can log on to chefkathleen.com and cry me a river. You'll get a cyberkick in the bloomers from me and the whole gang on the forums. If you need more support, work your way through your call list until you feel better. The point is to teach yourself how to work through Gloomy Gus guzzling, energy-sapping days. Do not use them as an excuse to retreat, nest, and eat. How do I know all about this? How do you *think* I know?

   If your depression is deeper than a one- or two-day funk, get help. You do not have to live with fear, anger, anxiety, pain, shame, or humiliation. It is your right to feel happy, productive, and healthy. There are resources, treatment, and medications that can help you achieve the peace and prosperity you genuinely deserve. Call your doctor or a counselor and make an appointment. When your car runs out of gas, you go to the gas station. Be strong and quick about this. You deserve the very best care. Think baby steps. Take one today. And repeat.

   Kathleen

FOOD **What do you *mean* you aren't eating five or six times a day yet?** Breakfast, lunch, and dinner and two snacks in between and *maybe* a nibbly bite after supper if you've got a few spare calories left to spend. Canned chickpeas tossed with couscous (or bulgur or quinoa), along with chopped tomatoes, crumbled feta, chopped mint, lemon juice, olive oil, salt, and pepper make a tasty take-to-work lunch or snack. If the queen's coming, serve it on butter lettuce leaves with heirloom tomatoes and garnish with lemon wedges and sprigs of mint.

FUN Pack up your baggage and take an emotional getaway! **Write down three activities that make you feel really happy and schedule them into your planner this week.** They don't have to be time hogs; think twenty minutes alone with the newest issue of *O* or Frisbee at the beach (if you're lucky enough to live near one) with your dog, or a trip through a fancy furniture store just to ooh and aah, plan and dream.

FITNESS **Chase the blues away with exercise.** It's widely known that exercise such as walking, swimming, cycling, and running can increase the amount of feel-good, mood-improving endorphins in your body by as much as 75 percent.

FOCUS Who do you 4-1-1 when you're feeling blue, lazy, unmotivated, or frustrated? Do they really help you? Do you feel good when you hang up the phone or are you more anxious than a whippet boarding a plane? Reevaluate your call list. **Make sure you're turning to people who offer the kind of support you truly need when you need it the most.**

Homework Assignment The I'll-never-lose-weight-so-why-try tryouts were this week, and you weren't chosen. I don't care if you feel like you've tried everything and it isn't working. You will continue to make progress when you stop making excuses and start focusing on where you can improve. Your assignment is to write down ways you get derailed and ways you can get back on track. Punch-bowl-size portions of cereal, keyboard bingeing, and torrid vending machine trysts are often the cause of "mysterious" plateaus. Is this you? Be honest.

YOUR GAME PLAN (STATE YOUR FOOD AND EXERCISE GOALS FOR THE WEEK)

Mango Shaved Ice

SERVES 6 *Americans eat an average of 45 pints of ice cream a year. Ice cream math can be grim news for waist watchers. A pint of Ben & Jerry's New York Super Fudge Chunk has 1240 calories and 80 grams of fat. Forty-five pints will set you back 55,800 calories and 3600 grams of fat. You could be looking at an almost 16-pound weight gain in just one year!*

Mango Shaved Ice can be made without an ice cream maker, which means it isn't ice-cream smooth, but it is ice-cream cool and refreshing and a lot better for you.

3 ripe mangoes (about 2¼ pounds), peeled, seeded, and cut into chunks or 2½ cups mango puree

¼ cup fresh lime juice (about 2 limes) or to taste

3 tablespoons superfine sugar or to taste

PLACE mango chunks in a blender or a food processor and blend until very smooth. Add lime juice and sugar. Pulse to combine.

POUR into a shallow flat baking dish or pan that will fit easily into your freezer. Freeze until frozen through, about 2 hours, stirring every half-hour to break up the ice crystals. For an authentic granita-style presentation, scrape shavings off with a fork and scoop into wine-glasses. Serve immediately.

■ *You can make shaved ice with any pureed fruit you like. Aim for 2½ cups of liquid, but if you end up with a little more or less, it doesn't matter.* ■ *Mango chunks are available in the freezer section of gourmet grocery stores and Trader Joe's. (Defrost slightly in a microwave before blending.)* ■ *You can find superfine sugar near regular granulated sugar in the baking aisle of your grocery store. Alternatively, you can use simple syrup, which is sold near the liquor because it's commonly used to sweeten cocktails. Read the nutrition label before you pour.*

A BLUE'S CLUE

A diet deficient in folic acid, the synthetic version of a B vitamin found naturally in foods, has been linked to depression. Foods containing folic acid may help in depression recovery. Mood-boosting foods include whole grains, dark leafy greens, avocado, chickpeas, black-eyed peas, peanuts, grapefruits, strawberries, and mangoes. How many of these foods can you work into your diet this week?

What I ate:

What I wish I hadn't:

What I did for exercise:

Tuesday

What I ate:

What I wish I hadn't:

What I did for exercise:

Wednesday

What I ate:

What I wish I hadn't:

What I did for exercise:

Thursday

What I ate:

What I wish I hadn't:

What I did for exercise:

Friday

What I ate:

What I wish I hadn't:

What I did for exercise:

Saturday

I REALLY FELT GREAT WHEN I

What I ate:

What I wish I hadn't:

I CAN GET BETTER AT

What I did for exercise:

Sunday

NEW FOODS I'M GOING TO TRY

What I ate:

NEXT WEEK I'M GOING TO

What I wish I hadn't:

What I did for exercise:

GIVE YOURSELF A GRADE
FOR THIS WEEK'S EFFORTS:

Boredom aside, sometimes there's a physical explanation for workout burnout and plateaus. Your body gets very efficient at repeating the same exercises day in and day out and learns how to do them using less and less energy as time goes by, which means you burn fewer calories and see fewer results. You can spin your wheels trying to prove that what you're currently doing is "enough" or wail to anyone who'll listen that your metabolism is "messed up" and cry in your coffee about how Suzie Size 2 doesn't have to work at this half as hard as you do, or you can give your workout routine the jump-start it needs and get back on track to lose the weight you want.

kd@chefkathleen.com

SUBJECT: EXCUSES NOT TO EXERCISE

FROM: Shaquita

TO: kd@chefkathleen.com

Dear Kathleen,
It's really hard to make time for exercise. I was going to the pool every day, but it seems like when I get busy, the first thing I do is cut out my exercise. How can I get back into it without feeling like I'm getting buried at work?

Shaquita

REPLY: NO BUTS! GET YOUR BUTT IN GEAR!

Dear Shaquita,
Two words: be selfish. The rule in finance is to pay yourself first. The rule in health is to get your workout in first. No ifs, ands, or buts about it. There will always be more work. Do you want to tackle your stack feeling healthy or feeling haggard? Your tombstone isn't going to say "I wish I went to work more."

Kathleen

FOOD Need a quick pick-me-up? You might not be getting enough protein. Skip the caffeine, chocolate, diet cola, and empty-calorie snacks. **Grab a pack of grocery-store sushi.** Twice the price of a Venti Full-Whip Mocha but *more* than twice the nutrition!

FUN Take the week off from your regular exercise routine and replace it with equivalent time doing something just as active or healing. Buy a Hula-Hoop, play Twister for an hour straight, but whatever you do, embrace the time off. **Embrace the change.**

FITNESS If you're not happy with your exercise payoff, change your routine. Explore your options. Instead of walking, sign up for swim classes. **If you've never tried yoga, might this be the week?** Pick up the latest class schedule at the gym, check out community classes, look up exercise DVDs online. Sometimes a change of pace is all it takes to build more lean muscle mass and rev up your metabolism.

FOCUS When I'm sick of exercising, I might spring for a session with a trainer or call up a friend and invite her to work out with me or I might just call my mother. She's always good for an earful on why I need to stop complaining and get back to work. "No one cares if you're bored, Kathleen. We're bored too. **Get back on your bike."**

Homework Assignment Write down three ways you can increase the intensity of your workouts or change them altogether. Walking with your grandma burns fewer calories than walking with a teenager in a hurry to "get this over with, Mom."

YOUR GAME PLAN (STATE YOUR FOOD AND EXERCISE GOALS FOR THE WEEK)

Mushroom Rice Stew

SERVES 4 TO 6 *Dried porcini mushrooms are a super-low-calorie ingredient that add a deep dimension of flavor that rivals the richest, most fattening beef stew you can think of, with none of the excess calories.*

1 **tablespoon butter**

2 **teaspoons olive oil**

1 **pound white or brown mushrooms, cut into quarters**

Coarse salt and cracked black pepper to taste

2 **stalks celery, cut into ¼- to ½-inch slices**

2 **large carrots, cut into ½-inch or bite-size pieces**

½ **large onion, diced**

½ **cup dried porcini mushrooms, crushed**

1 **bay leaf**

1 **tablespoon all-purpose flour**

¾ **cup dry red wine**

4 **cups low-sodium chicken or vegetable broth**

1 **14- or 15-ounce can ground peeled tomatoes**

¾ **cup brown rice**

3 **sprigs fresh thyme or 1 teaspoon dried**

HEAT butter and oil in a large heavy pot over medium-high heat until butter melts. Add the fresh mushrooms and cook, stirring often, until most of the liquid has evaporated, about 2 minutes. Season with salt and pepper and continue cooking for 2 minutes more.

ADD celery, carrots, onion, dried mushrooms, and bay leaf. Cook, stirring occasionally, until vegetables have softened, about 10 minutes. Add flour and cook, stirring, for 2 to 3 minutes. Add red wine, broth, and tomatoes. Bring to a boil and add rice. Bring back to a boil, immediately reduce to a strong simmer, and cook, uncovered, until rice is done, 25 to 35 minutes. Add thyme and cook for 2 minutes more. Remove bay leaf and serve.

■ *Dried mushrooms are available in Asian markets, in the gourmet section of most grocery stores, and often near the fresh mushrooms in the produce aisle.*

BURN OFF THAT CANDY BAR

In 30 minutes, a 150-pound woman can burn:

* 85 calories (one third of a candy bar), taking a leisurely walk at 2 miles per hour

* 112 calories (slightly less than half a candy bar), walking 3 miles per hour

* 170 calories (two thirds of that candy bar), walking briskly at 4 miles per hour

* A whopping 272 calories (the whole dang bar) jogging in place to her favorite TV show

What I ate:

What I wish I hadn't:

What I did for exercise:

Tuesday

What I ate:

What I wish I hadn't:

What I did for exercise:

Wednesday

What I ate:

What I wish I hadn't:

What I did for exercise:

Thursday

What I ate:

What I wish I hadn't:

What I did for exercise:

Friday

What I ate:

What I wish I hadn't:

What I did for exercise:

Saturday

I REALLY FELT GREAT WHEN I

What I ate:

What I wish I hadn't:

I CAN GET BETTER AT

What I did for exercise:

NEW FOODS I'M GOING TO TRY

Sunday

What I ate:

NEXT WEEK I'M GOING TO

What I wish I hadn't:

What I did for exercise:

GIVE YOURSELF A GRADE
FOR THIS WEEK'S EFFORTS:

WEEK 10

I'm *Sick* of Cooking, Kathleeeeen!

You think *you're* in a food rut. Sometimes I have to test recipes and cook all day. Food doesn't always have to be a source of entertainment, though I prefer to look forward to every meal. If you look for reasons to eat out or order carry-out all the time, you're more likely to consume excess, poor-quality calories void of proper nutrition. Cooking at home and eating foods that are good for you is the best way to control the quantity and quality of calories you're consuming. When you're in a culinary funk, review your goals, think about the message a positive change of attitude will send to loved ones, think out of the icebox, and dig in.

VEGGIES IN A HURRY

While you have the oven on, roast a veggie or two. Just about any veggie roasts in 15 to 25 minutes at 450°F. Toss them with a little olive oil, salt, and pepper. Spread them on a cookie sheet in a single layer and cook until fork-tender. Allow 15 minutes for asparagus, 20 to 25 minutes for broccoli florets or sliced sweet potatoes.

FOOD **The best food rut–buster I know is to open a cookbook, close your eyes, and pick a recipe.** Or buy something new at the grocery store: an unusual vegetable or a spice blend you haven't used before. One of my favorite recipes I discovered this way is sesame chili green beans. Heat 2 teaspoons sesame oil in a wok or skillet with minced red chili peppers or jalapeño and slivered garlic. Add steamed green beans, salt, and pepper to taste, and cook, tossing often, until just warm, about 2 minutes.

FUN Take a cooking class. Check your Sunday paper or call a local kitchen store to find out what's coming up. **Cooking classes are a great way to get out, meet new people, and learn something really fun.** If you won't do that, invite some friends over and cook something you've always wanted to try or have a potluck and ask everyone to bring a new healthy recipe.

FITNESS **If the scale's stuck, you need to move more and/or eat less.** I find that if I work in a few more soup-and-salad meals and increase the intensity of my cardio workouts, it's enough to get the scale inching back in the right direction.

FOCUS You can't master cooking at home if you don't put any effort into it. **Pretend you're trying out to be the star of your own cooking show.** Figure out how to make cooking fun for your audience, and chances are you'll have a blast.

Homework Assignment Choose three recipes from this book. Make

a shopping list. Prepare all three by Friday. Choose a reward from your kitchen wish list that's posted on your fridge. It can be yours before the week's out.

YOUR GAME PLAN (STATE YOUR FOOD AND EXERCISE GOALS FOR THE WEEK)

Pan-Fried Eggplant with Cilantro and Lime

SERVES 4 *You'll have to fry the eggplant in batches using mostly olive oil cooking spray, but each time you place a new batch of eggplant in the pan, add a ½ teaspoon sesame oil.*

1 **large eggplant, peeled and cut crosswise into ½-inch-thick slices**
 Olive oil spray
1½ **teaspoons sesame oil**
 Coarse salt and cracked black pepper
¼ **cup fresh lime juice**
½ **cup loosely packed, coarsely chopped fresh cilantro**

LAYER eggplant slices on a microwave-proof plate. Cover tightly with plastic wrap and microwave on high for 4 minutes.

PLACE a large nonstick pan over medium heat and, when hot but not smoking, add a coating of olive oil spray and ½ teaspoon sesame oil. Cover pan bottom with a single layer of eggplant slices. Season with salt and pepper and cook until golden brown, turning once, about 3 minutes per side, spraying pan with oil during cooking if necessary.

AS soon as eggplant is cooked, transfer to a serving platter. Continue until all eggplant is cooked. Pour lime juice over platter, sprinkle with cilantro, and serve.

■ *For a different dish, use olive oil instead of sesame oil, and balsamic vinegar and basil in place of the lime and cilantro.*

Monday

What I ate:

What I wish I hadn't:

What I did for exercise:

Tuesday

What I ate:

What I wish I hadn't:

What I did for exercise:

Wednesday

What I ate:

What I wish I hadn't:

What I did for exercise:

Thursday

What I ate:

What I wish I hadn't:

What I did for exercise:

Friday

What I ate:

What I wish I hadn't:

What I did for exercise:

Saturday

What I ate:

What I wish I hadn't:

What I did for exercise:

I REALLY FELT GREAT WHEN I

I CAN GET BETTER AT

NEW FOODS I'M GOING TO TRY

Sunday

What I ate:

What I wish I hadn't:

What I did for exercise:

NEXT WEEK I'M GOING TO

GIVE YOURSELF A GRADE
FOR THIS WEEK'S EFFORTS:

WEEK 11
Know What You're Fighting For

"I want to lose weight" is vague. "I want to weigh what I did in college" is ridiculous unless the ink on your diploma is still wet. And "I want to fit into my wedding dress" is just as self-defeating. "I want to lose a pound by Saturday" is succinct, something you can focus on. It's hard to make a game plan when you're not absolutely clear on what you're working toward, and it's really hard to stay motivated without prizes, payoffs, and rewards. Set small, realistic, achievable goals, create weekly game plans you can stick to, collect rewards along the way, and you will lose this weight and improve your overall health once and for all.

kd@chefkathleen.com

SUBJECT: I'M BORED!
FROM: Paige
TO: kd@chefkathleen.com

Dear Kathleen,
I'm really bored with my exercise routine. I switch my routine, but it's not enough. What to do?
   Paige

REPLY: BECOME A CHARITY CASE

Dear Paige,
Sign up for a charity fitness event that makes you say "There's no way I could *ever* do that." Create a workout plan designed to get you in shape for the big event. Plot every day's workout from now until the starting gun goes pop. Consult a trainer if that's what it takes. Your workouts will have a new focus. The sense of urgency to get in race-day shape will motivate you, and knowing people are counting on you will keep you going.
   Kathleen

FOOD Slim down your side dishes, and you'll slim down too. **This week, forgo the scoop of mac and cheese.** Hold the buttery mashed potatoes and forget about stuffing and gravy. Instead, include a microwaved or quick roasted veggie and a salad with every evening meal. A quick dressing of balsamic vinegar whisked together with whole-grain mustard and a sprinkling of chopped herbs such as rosemary, thyme, or oregano is a great way to perk up roasted vegetables.

FUN Monday through Friday, small rewards are important, but what do you want to see when Monty Hall opens door number one? **Write down your ultimate weight-loss goal and write down your reward.** Spend free moments researching the cruise of your dreams, your fantasy car, or whatever it is you've chosen to be your goal-weight Grand Prize.

FITNESS **Are you working a wee bit harder than you did last week?** Are you putting in stay-the-same sessions or goal-weight performances? Stay at rock bottom awhile longer or climb up and out for good. Five extra minutes six days this week is thirty minutes extra this week. Burn 149 calories belly dancing, 165 calories walking, or 397 calories riding your bike, and you're on your way to easy-to-achieve permanent weight loss. Now that's magic!

FOCUS Repeat after me, **"Do the work, and you will reach your goals."**

Homework Assignment Identify three things you want to accomplish by Saturday and make a list of the behaviors that will ensure success. Be specific. Check your calendar to identify obstacles and events that have the potential to throw you off course. Post your game plan next to a list of rewards on your fridge. It's hard to slip into denial or "forget" your game plan when it's posted for all the world to see.

YOUR GAME PLAN (STATE YOUR FOOD AND EXERCISE GOALS FOR THE WEEK)

Roasted Sweet Potato and Beet Salad in Creamy Buttermilk Dressing

SERVES 4 *It's important that the beets are half the size of the sweet potatoes, so they are done at the same time. Don't salt the dressing until after you add the roasted vegetables. Peel everything with a vegetable peeler. If you like your beets more tender, cut them smaller.*

2 **small sweet potatoes (about 1¾ pounds), peeled and cut into ½-inch chunks**

3 **medium beets (about 1½ pounds), peeled and cut into ½-inch chunks**

1 **tablespoon olive oil**

Coarse salt and cracked black pepper to taste

½ **cup low-fat buttermilk**

1 **tablespoon Dijon mustard**

1 **garlic clove, minced**

1 **teaspoon minced fresh thyme or ½ teaspoon dried**

PREHEAT oven to 450°F. Place sweet potatoes, beets, and olive oil in a plastic bag or large bowl and shake or stir until well coated. Pour sweet potatoes and beets onto a cookie sheet. Season with salt and pepper and place in oven. Cook, turning once, for 25 to 35 minutes, or until cooked through and fork-tender. Cool slightly.

MEANWHILE, in a large salad bowl, whisk together buttermilk, mustard, garlic, and thyme. Add sweet potatoes and beets to bowl and toss until well coated. Taste and adjust seasonings with salt and pepper and serve.

■ *The dressing is also great with dill in place of thyme.*

3 REASONS TO WORK SWEET POTATOES INTO YOUR DIET

1. Sweet potatoes have more fiber than oatmeal. Fiber fills you up and keeps you feeling "full" longer. A dieter's dream!

2. Sweet potatoes are virtually fat-free, cholesterol-free, and very low in sodium. A medium sweet potato has just 118 calories.

3. One cup of cooked sweet potatoes provides 30 milligrams of beta-carotene (vitamin A). It would take 23 cups of broccoli to provide the same amount.

Monday

What I ate:

What I wish I hadn't:

What I did for exercise:

Tuesday

What I ate:

What I wish I hadn't:

What I did for exercise:

Wednesday

What I ate:

What I wish I hadn't:

What I did for exercise:

Thursday

What I ate:

What I wish I hadn't:

What I did for exercise:

Friday

What I ate:

What I wish I hadn't:

What I did for exercise:

REPORT CARD

I REALLY FELT GREAT WHEN I

I CAN GET BETTER AT

NEW FOODS I'M GOING TO TRY

NEXT WEEK I'M GOING TO

GIVE YOURSELF A GRADE
FOR THIS WEEK'S EFFORTS:

Saturday

What I ate:

What I wish I hadn't:

What I did for exercise:

Sunday

What I ate:

What I wish I hadn't:

What I did for exercise:

I lost the first chunk of weight by scaling back on foods I had no business eating and by working in more foods I hadn't eaten since my mother was serving up the pureed versions from Gerber jars. And then the scale stood still. To make the needle budge and trim more pudge, I had to come to terms with the fact that size matters. Dig out the nutrition books, the measuring cups and spoons, and a good old kitchen scale. Use them for a couple of weeks until you get used to proper portions.

kd@chefkathleen.com

SUBJECT: NUMBERS CHALLENGED

FROM: Fannie

TO: kd@chefkathleen.com

Dear Kathleen,
I don't want to count calories because it's tedious, and I just don't have that kind of time. How can I learn about serving sizes and portions?

Fannie (No Fan of Numbers)

REPLY: STACK THE DECK IN YOUR FAVOR

Dear Fannie,
I learned early on that the suggested-serving-size people work for the stick-girl brigade. I've taken matters into my own hands by paying attention to the calories of the actual servings I consume. My sister Carol, fresh out of weight-loss basic training, recently dropped her first 20 pounds and has this to say on the subject: "Take charge of yourself. Have decks of cards all over to remind you of what a proper serving of meat is supposed to look like, or bite the bullet and splurge on a kitchen scale. You need to know that an ounce of cheese looks like an anorexic domino. And that an ounce of nuts is smaller than the nanoportion of peanuts they used to hand out in coach class."

Learn to be hungry. It gets easier: I promise. In the meantime, fill up on "free" foods: regular veggies, steamed veggies, raw veggies, steamed veggies, raw . . .

Kathleen

FOOD From Mom's lips to your ears: don't make a recipe that serves 4 to 6 people if there are only two of you and you won't freeze the leftovers. **As a general rule, purchase 4 ounces of protein per person.** I hunt for recipes that serve four and have lots of vegetables and cut the protein back to serve two.

FUN Lose weight talking on the phone! **Walk around like a maniac the whole time, and you'll burn calories.** The moral of the story—build more movement into your day, and your efforts will pay off in the way of permanent weight loss. Slow and steady wins the race!

FITNESS Lose up to 6½ pounds a year by parking ten minutes from your office and walking the distance to work. **A 150-pound woman can burn up to 45 calories per 10-minute trip.** If you work five days a week, that's 22,499 calories burned for the year and a trip to the tailor to get every last pair of pants taken in.

FOCUS Identify someone in your life you admire who has just as crazy a schedule as you but somehow manages to work in exercise. Ask her how she does it. **Focus on what you can do tomorrow to get in thirty minutes of exercise before bedtime.** Keep your focus on tomorrow, especially if the big picture overwhelms you. Plan your reward in advance. Collect it immediately upon crossing the finish line.

Homework Assignment Go to mypyramid.gov and surf through the site until you feel like a portion-control expert.

YOUR GAME PLAN (STATE YOUR FOOD AND EXERCISE GOALS FOR THE WEEK)

Spinach, Ham, and Cheddar Pancakes

SERVES 4 TO 5; MAKES 10 PANCAKES *These pancakes are delightful, something I've served at cocktail parties, for Sunday brunch, and Sunday supper. They're light yet substantial. A garden salad is all you need to round out the meal.*

8 **large egg whites**

2 **large eggs**

1 **teaspoon dried thyme**

Half a 10-ounce bag prewashed baby spinach (about 4 cups), large leaves halved

½ **pound ham, diced small**

2 **ounces sharp cheddar cheese, grated**

2 **teaspoons olive oil**

1 **small onion, thinly sliced**

IN a large bowl, whisk together egg whites and eggs. Stir in thyme, spinach, ham, and cheese.

HEAT oil in a large nonstick skillet over medium-high heat until hot but not smoking. Add onion and cook, stirring occasionally until wilted and golden, 4 to 5 minutes. Add to egg mixture and stir until combined.

WIPE out pan. Heat over medium-high heat. For each pancake, pour ¼ cup egg mixture into skillet and cook for 2 minutes, or until golden brown. Turn pancakes and cook until other side is golden brown, about 2 minutes more. Serve immediately.

■ *You can also serve these pancakes with yogurt, to which you've added some fresh chopped mint.*

Monday

What I ate:

What I wish I hadn't:

What I did for exercise:

Tuesday

What I ate:

What I wish I hadn't:

What I did for exercise:

Wednesday

What I ate:

What I wish I hadn't:

What I did for exercise:

Thursday

What I ate:

What I wish I hadn't:

What I did for exercise:

Friday

What I ate:

What I wish I hadn't:

What I did for exercise:

Saturday

I REALLY FELT GREAT WHEN I

I CAN GET BETTER AT

NEW FOODS I'M GOING TO TRY

NEXT WEEK I'M GOING TO

GIVE YOURSELF A GRADE
FOR THIS WEEK'S EFFORTS:

What I ate:

What I wish I hadn't:

What I did for exercise:

Sunday

What I ate:

What I wish I hadn't:

What I did for exercise:

I've spent a lot of time in doctors' offices lately. The message to eat right is never quite as strong as when you're staring at yourself in a mirror bathed in glaring fluorescent lighting and dressed in a medical gray examining gown big enough to drape a family of manatees. Do you really want to spend the rest of your life in waiting rooms stocked with bad magazines published several *years* before your appointment? Prevention goes down a whole lot easier than some of the remedies you have no choice but to try.

kd@chefkathleen.com

SUBJECT: SLIP SLIDING AWAY
FROM: Holly
TO: kd@chefkathleen.com

Dear Kathleen,
I am trying to lose weight and have been struggling. I start out doing really well, but then one slip-up and it all goes downhill.
  Holly

REPLY: GIVE UP GIVING UP

Dear Holly,
When it all goes downhill, I'm guessing that you go back to your old eating habits and stop exercising? That's a pretty big payoff for one slip-up. My payment for failing used to be big Bertha binges until I realized I was failing in anticipation of the boohoo buffets. Give up giving up. A slip-up is an opportunity to level the playing field. The best way to rebound is to counteract less than ideal behavior with better behavior. Extra dessert is an extra walk. Extra food means extra exercise. Take things one behavioral change at a time. Good luck, Holly. You can do this!
  Kathleen

FOOD Think about the worst health crisis of your life. Think about how the food you've consumed throughout your life may have affected that crisis before, during, and after. **Food is your first line of defense.** It is medicine. It is fuel. It can build you up or tear you down. Whatcha having for supper? Whole-wheat spaghetti with olive oil, hot pepper, slivered garlic, lemon juice and zest, capers, and arugula topped with a little freshly grated Parmesan cheese is split-second quick.

FUN **Take a culinary field trip.** Visit a farmers' market, go to a bookstore and look at cookbooks, visit a vegetable garden, buy some lettuce seeds and plant them, go to Penzeys.com and order a handful of freshly ground herbs and spices.

FITNESS Walk up stairs for ten minutes and burn 91 calories. **What goes up must come down.** Walking down burns another 45. Do that five days a week for a year, over and above your regular exercise, and you can kiss up to 10 pounds bye-bye!

FOCUS If you haven't had a health scare, you're truly blessed. Do not take this good fortune for granted. Don't kid yourself into thinking that poor eating and exercise habits will never catch up with you just because so far you haven't been confined to a suite in the cardiac ward and forced to suck Jell-O through a straw. **Your body cannot run indefinitely on junk, and it's not going to reward you for not exercising.** Clean up your act a little bit each day.

Homework Assignment Make a list of all the stuff you eat that would cause a dietician's eyeballs to roll clear out of her head. Next to each food item, write down how often you consume it. Now go through the list again, pretend you're hooked up to a lie detector machine, and adjust your answers accordingly. Next add up the number of junk calories you consume daily. Multiply that number by 365. Now divide it by 3500 (the number of calories in a pound). How many extra pounds are you needlessly stuffing into your jeans every year?

YOUR GAME PLAN (STATE YOUR FOOD AND EXERCISE GOALS FOR THE WEEK)

Thai Beef Salad

SERVES 4 *You can roll up this salad into flour or corn tortillas and call them beef tacos.*

Flank steak, a lean cut, is usually sold in 1-pound pieces or larger, which means you'll have more meat than you need for this recipe. Cook it all up at once and save the leftovers for steak salads and sandwiches or freeze half of it for later.

¼ **cup fresh lime juice**

¼ **cup fresh orange juice**

1 **tablespoon fish sauce**

2 **tablespoons rice wine vinegar**

1 **tablespoon dark brown sugar**

1 **tablespoon (more or less), grated jalapeño pepper**

5 **scallions, white and some green parts, very thinly sliced**

8 **cups very thinly sliced napa cabbage (about ½ large head)**

2 **cups grated carrots (from a 10-ounce bag)**

1 **cup loosely packed, coarsely chopped fresh mint**

1 **cup loosely packed, coarsely chopped fresh cilantro**

½ **pound flank steak**

Coarse salt and cracked black pepper

PREHEAT oven broiler to high. In a bowl large enough to hold the salad, whisk together lime juice, orange juice, fish sauce, vinegar, brown sugar, and jalapeño. Add scallions.

TOSS together cabbage, carrots, mint, and cilantro in same bowl.

SEASON meat with salt and pepper, put on broiler pan, and place under the broiler. Broil, turning once, until done to your liking, 5 to 6 minutes per side for medium-rare, 8 minutes for medium, 9 to 10 minutes for well done. (Alternatively, you can grill in a grill pan by lightly oiling the steak, using about ½ teaspoon of olive oil per side. Season with salt and pepper and cook on high as above.)

REMOVE meat to a cutting board and let rest for 10 minutes before slicing very thin across grain. Add to bowl with cabbage. Toss to coat evenly with dressing and serve.

NAPA CABBAGE

Napa cabbage can be found in most grocery stores near the lettuces or cabbage. A head of napa is shaped like a head of romaine, but the leaves are much paler green and the core and stalks are white. Napa contains cancer-fighting phytochemicals, fiber, vitamin C, and a small amount of folate. Because the leaves are the perfect host for scrumptious dressings, raw napa cabbage is wonderful in salads and quick slaws. You can also sauté, steam, or use in stir-fries. Don't buy cabbage pre-cut because once the head is sliced the amount of vitamin C starts to diminish.

Monday

What I ate:

What I wish I hadn't:

What I did for exercise:

Tuesday

What I ate:

What I wish I hadn't:

What I did for exercise:

Wednesday

What I ate:

What I wish I hadn't:

What I did for exercise:

Thursday

What I ate:

What I wish I hadn't:

What I did for exercise:

Friday

What I ate:

What I wish I hadn't:

What I did for exercise:

Saturday

REPORT CARD

I REALLY FELT GREAT WHEN I

I CAN GET BETTER AT

NEW FOODS I'M GOING TO TRY

NEXT WEEK I'M GOING TO

GIVE YOURSELF A GRADE
FOR THIS WEEK'S EFFORTS:

What I ate:

What I wish I hadn't:

What I did for exercise:

Sunday

What I ate:

What I wish I hadn't:

What I did for exercise:

Skip Folding Laundry, but Don't Skip Meals

So busy you skip meals? Send your children off to school every day this week without breakfast. Tell them they're forbidden to eat until dinnertime. Naturally they'll perform better in school than they ever have. Yeah, right.

Seriously, now: put as much time into preparing and planning your own meals as you do those of your loved ones.

kd@chefkathleen.com

SUBJECT: TOO BUSY FOR BREAKFAST

FROM: Lori
TO: kd@chefkathleen.com

Dear Kathleen,
My family is too busy to eat break-fast. The kids are always running late, which means I'm always running late. I usually give them cereal bars or stop at a drive-through. I feel very guilty, but I don't know how to change this. They refuse to eat anything healthy.
Lori

REPLY: GIVE YOUR KIDS AN INCENTIVE

Dear Lori,
If you have time for drive-through, you have time for sit-down. I understand it can take some kids an hour to eat four Wheaties, but where there's a will there's a way. Announce to your family that starting on Monday, it's their responsibility to eat a healthy breakfast before school. Get rid of all the junk breakfast foods in the house and stock up on whole-grain cereals, oatmeal, cream of wheat, whole-grain English muffins, regular-size bagels and bread, peanut butter and all-fruit jam.

If your kids *must* eat in the car, buy some disposable coffee cups, plastic spoons, and napkins or wipes for eating cereal. Peanut butter and jelly sandwiches travel too. Make up some breakfast grab bags — package whole-grain cereals, dried fruits, and nuts in little bags. One healthy breakfast wins a quarter, or fifteen minutes more outside playtime after dinner, or something else meaningful. And five days wins your kids something they "really want."
Kathleen

FOOD **No time to cook?** Whip up a batch of chili on the run and a sesame, orange, and spinach salad. Here's your shopping list: ½ pound ground white-meat chicken or very lean ground beef, 1 (28-ounce) can ground peeled tomatoes, 2 (15-ounce) cans, no-sodium black beans, 1 package taco seasoning mix, low-sodium tomato juice or chicken broth (optional), 3 oranges or clementines, 1 (10-ounce) bag baby spinach, sliced raw almonds, 1 bottle low-calorie Asian Sesame Salad Dressing.

Brown meat, add tomatoes, beans, and half the taco seasoning. Mix to taste. Add just enough water, tomato juice, or chicken broth to thin out to the consistency you like.

For the salad, peel oranges and separate them into sections, place in a large salad bowl with spinach, ¼ cup almonds, and 3 tablespoons dressing. Gently toss to coat evenly. Taste and adjust seasonings with more dressing if necessary.

FUN **Splurge on healthy gourmet-to-go from your grocery store one night this week.**

FITNESS Topped with steamed veggies or salsa, a baked potato is a smart and easy choice to have the night before a race or after a tough workout. Potatoes are a great, easily digestible source of muscle-fueling carbohydrates. **According to the Potato Board, one medium-size potato contains zero fat, 26 grams of carbohydrates, and only about 100 calories.** Eaten with the skin, the potato is an excellent source of vitamin C, potassium, and fiber.

FOCUS Plan tomorrow's speedy supper. **Make a shopping list and stock up.** The act of doing so will program you to stay on track. When urge-to-carryout beckons, healthy-homemade will dismiss her without a second thought.

Homework Assignment Decide that you will not skip a single meal this week. Visualize yourself eating meals you usually skip. If you eat a bowl of cereal with fruit every day for breakfast, a turkey sandwich every day for lunch, and low-sodium canned soup with a side salad every night, so what if you're bored? Look at what you've accomplished. Branch out and upgrade your meals from there.

YOUR GAME PLAN (STATE YOUR FOOD AND EXERCISE GOALS FOR THE WEEK)

Creamy Buttermilk Coleslaw

SERVES 6 TO 8 *For the most part, I like my coleslaw pretty plain. But if you want to work in a few servings of fruits or veggies, consider adding very thinly sliced onion or scallion, thinly sliced red or green peppers, grated apple, pineapple chunks, or red or green grapes, halved. This recipe calls for you to season the cabbage with a little bit of salt and to let it sit in a colander for an hour or all day, so plan ahead.*

 1 **pound napa cabbage, very thinly sliced (about 6 cups)**
 ½ **teaspoon coarse salt**
 ½ **cup low-fat buttermilk**
 2 **tablespoons low-fat plain yogurt**
 2 **tablespoons low-fat mayonnaise**
 1 **tablespoon honey Dijon mustard**
 1 **teaspoon cider vinegar**
 2 **teaspoons grated fresh ginger**
    Grated zest of 1 lime
    Cracked black pepper
 1½ **cups shredded carrots (available pregrated in bags)**
 ½ **cup loosely packed, coarsely chopped fresh cilantro**

PLACE cabbage in a colander set in sink. Sprinkle with salt, toss to coat evenly.

WHILE cabbage is wilting, in a bowl you'll serve salad in, whisk together buttermilk, yogurt, mayonnaise, mustard, cider vinegar, ginger, and lime zest. Add pepper to taste. Toss in carrots and cilantro.

PAT cabbage dry, add to salad; toss to coat evenly. Serve or refrigerate for 30 minutes and serve cold.

ZERO-PREP SALAD TOPPINGS AND THEIR CALORIC VIRTUES

Asparagus (5 spears)
18 CALORIES

Beets (½ cup sliced)
30 CALORIES

Broccoli (½ cup florets)
12 CALORIES

Cantaloupe
(one quarter of 1 medium)
48 CALORIES

Carrots (1 cup grated)
60 CALORIES

Corn off the cob
(½ cup kernels)
66 CALORIES

Cucumber (½ cup sliced)
7 CALORIES

Grapes (1 cup)
114 CALORIES

Honeydew
(one quarter of 1 medium)
88 CALORIES

Mango (1 cup cubed)
107 CALORIES

Orange (1 medium)
62 CALORIES

Peas (½ cup)
59 CALORIES

**Peppers, red, yellow,
orange, or green**
(½ cup diced)
20 CALORIES

Tomatoes (½ cup chopped)
19 CALORIES

Zucchini (½ cup cubed)
9 CALORIES

What I ate:

What I wish I hadn't:

What I did for exercise:

What I ate:

What I wish I hadn't:

What I did for exercise:

Wednesday

What I ate:

What I wish I hadn't:

What I did for exercise:

Thursday

What I ate:

What I wish I hadn't:

What I did for exercise:

Friday

What I ate:

What I wish I hadn't:

What I did for exercise:

REPORT CARD

I REALLY FELT GREAT WHEN I

I CAN GET BETTER AT

NEW FOODS I'M GOING TO TRY

NEXT WEEK I'M GOING TO

GIVE YOURSELF A GRADE
FOR THIS WEEK'S EFFORTS:

Saturday

What I ate:

What I wish I hadn't:

What I did for exercise:

Sunday

What I ate:

What I wish I hadn't:

What I did for exercise:

Eat at the table. It's the thing with four legs and a bunch of chairs gathered around it. I'm sure you have one, or at least a decent stand-in. Eating in bed, eating in your car, eating at your computer, eating in front of the television, eating at your desk, and eating in your bathtub are sure-fire ways to gain weight, keep gaining weight, and ensure that you never reach your goals. When was the last time you gathered the family around the table and ate an entire bag of chips, a carton of dip, a box of cookies, and a half gallon of ice cream? Eating at the table is a time to relax and nurture your body and relationships. Keep things light and fun.

kd@chefkathleen.com

SUBJECT: NO TIME FOR TOGETHERNESS

FROM: Dennise

TO: kd@chefkathleen.com

Dear Kathleen,
When I was young, my family ate dinner together every night. But my husband and I have three children — eight, eleven, and fourteen — and it seems as if we never sit down to eat together. I'm constantly shuttling them around, and my husband works late a lot. What can I do?
Dennise

REPLY: TRY FOR ONCE A WEEK

Dear Dennise,
Start with a goal of sitting down together once a week. Get your husband to commit to a night he can be home at dinnertime. Post the menu on the refrigerator. Clear everyone's schedule. Choose family-favorite foods. Keep the conversation light and lively, no tough subjects. Before you leave the table, ask what everyone would like for dinner at the next family night. Ask your husband what night will work for him. In the future, when it comes time to sign up for activities, build in family time before making choices.
Kathleen

FOOD **Pack up your family and a picnic supper and head out to the nearest park.** You can make chicken salad sandwich wraps in a hurry using a preroasted chicken. Discard the skin and bones, dice up the meat, and toss with celery, carrots, onion, dill, and equal parts low-fat mayonnaise and no-fat Greek-style yogurt. Spread salad in whole-wheat tortillas layered with thin tomato slices. Cook some green beans in the microwave and toss with a low-cal dressing. You can buy pineapple and melon already cut into chunks, and strawberries and blueberries are pop-in-your-mouth ready to go!

FUN **Give your kitchen table a makeover.** Go to T. J. Maxx or Target and look for some new table linens—wash-and-wear festive place mats and napkins. Flea market and garage sale finds—antique salt and pepper shakers, porcelain pitchers, or a Carnival glass vase—make great centerpieces.

FITNESS The gym isn't the only place you can get a good workout this week. **If your kitchen needs a facelift, first give it a good top-to-bottom scrubbing.** Clean the woodwork, replace the curtains, swap out the knickknacks. Kitchen table and chairs in need of a new paint job? Carve out the time to strip and repaint them. It's great fun, rewarding, and it's free therapy!

FOCUS Eating at the table is an Ozzie-and-Harriet ideal that for some of us will require a lot more work than others. **Create forward movement daily.** Don't give up or give in.

Homework Assignment Keep track of how many times you eat at the table this week. When you don't eat sitting down at the table, write down why and post it on the refrigerator for all the world to see. Read it every single time you head toward the fridge. Put some real thought into this process. The act of sitting down probably means you're taking really good care of yourself and your family by carving out time to enjoy the food, family, friends, and conversation. Not sitting down can mean the opposite. Or that your money was spent on things other than chairs.

YOUR GAME PLAN (STATE YOUR FOOD AND EXERCISE GOALS FOR THE WEEK)

Pasta with Roasted Fennel, Onion, and Tomatoes with Parmesan

SERVES 4 *You may want to add some water to the pan of roasted vegetables just before you add the pasta if the veggies look a little dry (save about a cup of the pasta water for this purpose). If you add the water when the veggies come out of the oven, all those delicious nibbly brown roasty bits clinging to the pan bottom and sides will become part of the sauce. Using a mandoline will cut prep time in half.*

2 medium heads fennel, halved, cored, and thinly sliced

½ large onion, sliced the same thickness as the fennel

1 pint cherry tomatoes

2 teaspoons olive oil
  Coarse salt

½ pound pasta noodles, such as penne or ziti
  Cracked black pepper

4 tablespoons grated Parmesan cheese

3 tablespoons chopped fresh basil

PREHEAT oven to 425°F. Place fennel, onion, tomatoes, olive oil, and salt in a large baking dish or baking sheet with sides. Toss to coat evenly. Let stand for 10 minutes so the salt has time to pull some moisture from fennel. Bake, stirring once at halfway point, until fennel and onions are softened and cooked through, about 25 minutes.

MEANWHILE, cook pasta in a large pot of boiling salted water until al dente. Drain and set aside. When vegetables are done, pour noodles into pan with veggies and add cheese and basil. Season with salt and pepper to taste and serve.

WHAT MAKES KIDS HAPPY?

According to Nick Stinnett and John Defrain, authors of *Secrets of Strong Families*, when 1500 school-age children were asked, "What do you think makes a happy family?" the children didn't list money, cars, big homes, or televisions. The answer they gave most was doing things together.

What I ate:

What I wish I hadn't:

What I did for exercise:

Tuesday

What I ate:

What I wish I hadn't:

What I did for exercise:

Wednesday

What I ate:

What I wish I hadn't:

What I did for exercise:

Thursday

What I ate:

What I wish I hadn't:

What I did for exercise:

Friday

What I ate:

What I wish I hadn't:

What I did for exercise:

REPORT CARD

I REALLY FELT GREAT WHEN I

I CAN GET BETTER AT

NEW FOODS I'M GOING TO TRY

NEXT WEEK I'M GOING TO

GIVE YOURSELF A GRADE
FOR THIS WEEK'S EFFORTS:

What I ate:

What I wish I hadn't:

What I did for exercise:

Sunday

What I ate:

What I wish I hadn't:

What I did for exercise:

The only way to mayday yourself back to healthy eating is to enter the Witness Protection Program. Restrict the consumption of all junk foods to occasions when you are in the presence of people who will stare you down like a mother shooing a stranger away from her baby carriage. I allow myself to have the foods I want, but I stick to my hard-and-fast rule of consuming them in front of anti-enablers. Who wants to dodge eye darts when you're polishing off a pint of melted-to-the-perfect-point chocolate ice cream?

kd@chefkathleen.com

SUBJECT: JUNK FOOD ENVY-ITIS

FROM: Aimee
TO: kd@chefkathleen.com

Dear Kathleen,
I am trying to lose weight, but my husband and kids don't need to. I wish we didn't have any junk in the house, but I can't deny them. It's really hard for me to resist things, especially when they're having a snack or dessert. What would you do?

Aimee

REPLY: LOSE THE JUNK FOOD

Dear Aimee,
One way to look at your situation is to define what it is that you think you'd be denying them by keeping junk food out of the house. Sugar highs? Trans-fat fests? Sodium overload? Calories that don't serve their nutritional needs?

Think about how many times a day you have the opportunity to consume junk food away from home. It's everywhere. Your family has plenty of opportunities too. There's no reason to stock junk food in the house, especially if it's causing you anxiety. Don't put yourself in situations you don't have the skills to cope with. Eliminate the situations.

Kathleen

FOOD Make a mental list of party-eating enablers. Decide that you will not eat junk with them ever again. **No one can make you eat what you don't want to eat.** The first step to stopping this behavior is deciding that you will change. Take small steps daily toward achieving this goal. For a quick party potluck dessert, toss orange sections and orange juice with strawberry halves, melon chunks, pineapple chunks, grapes, blueberries (and raspberries if you're feeling rich), and the juice of a lemon. Serve plain or in wineglasses with a dollop of yogurt and a sprig of mint.

FUN For that three-day getaway state of relaxation minus the credit card debt, visit a really fancy nursery on a day you can take your time and browse. **In the winter when I'm feeling blue, I go to a nearby nursery that has a huge greenhouse filled with tropical plants.** I've never left less than inspired, soothed, and invigorated. And it's free!

FITNESS Before you resume or begin outdoor fitness routines this season, evaluate your fitness wardrobe. **Proper-fitting sport-appropriate shoes are very important.** Wear wet-dry or breathable fabrics so you're comfortable throughout your workout. Wear sunscreen and don't forget to protect the back of your neck, the backs of your hands, and your lips.

FOCUS **As team captain, it's up to you to identify who can join you in the Witness Protection safe house.** Determine who in your life is going to make you feel safe enough to have your treats but will step in when necessary and encourage you to stay on track in a way that's meaningful and helpful.

Homework Assignment

Homework Assignment Pound-Pal-proof your cupboards. If you're not ready to ditch everything, ditch something. Make a concentrated effort to replace bad foods with better foods. Put food items that you're not ready to banish from your house entirely out of sight, out of mind. Wrap the chocolate chips in tin foil and bind them with duct tape all the way around the package so tight that a game show contestant couldn't get them open in time to win the trip to Bermuda. Shove them in a coffee can and put them in the back of a cupboard you have to drag out a ladder to access.

YOUR GAME PLAN (STATE YOUR FOOD AND EXERCISE GOALS FOR THE WEEK)

Sea Salt–Baked French Fries

SERVES 4 *These fries have a deep, satisfying quality. You don't have to use sea salt; it has wonderful flavor, but use kosher salt if you can't get it. Tossing the fries with fresh herbs when they come out of the oven offers endless possibilities, especially in the summertime.*

2 **large baking potatoes, peeled and cut into french fry–like sticks**

2 **teaspoons peanut oil**

1 **teaspoon sesame oil**

 Sea salt to taste

1 **teaspoon paprika**

PREHEAT oven to 425°F. Place potato sticks in a bowl or 1-gallon plastic bag. Add 1 teaspoon peanut oil and sesame oil. Toss until well coated. Spread remaining peanut oil on a rimmed cookie sheet. Pour potatoes onto cookie sheet in a single layer. Season with salt and paprika.

COOK, turning once at the halfway point with a metal spatula, until golden brown, 30 to 35 minutes. Serve immediately.

■ *To cut a potato into french fries, slice it in half lengthwise. Lay each potato half cut side down on the cutting board. Cut each half into ¾-inch-thick lengthwise slices. Turn the stack of slices onto their sides and cut into ¾-inch-thick lengthwise strips, or french fries. If you like crunchier fries, cut them thinner.* ■ *Try different spices in place of the paprika.*

Monday

What I ate:

What I wish I hadn't:

What I did for exercise:

Tuesday

What I ate:

What I wish I hadn't:

What I did for exercise:

Wednesday

What I ate:

What I wish I hadn't:

What I did for exercise:

Thursday

What I ate:

What I wish I hadn't:

What I did for exercise:

Friday

What I ate:

What I wish I hadn't:

What I did for exercise:

Saturday

I REALLY FELT GREAT WHEN I

What I ate:

What I wish I hadn't:

I CAN GET BETTER AT

What I did for exercise:

NEW FOODS I'M GOING TO TRY

Sunday

What I ate:

What I wish I hadn't:

NEXT WEEK I'M GOING TO

What I did for exercise:

GIVE YOURSELF A GRADE
FOR THIS WEEK'S EFFORTS:

WEEK 17
Eat Out Less, Lose Weight Now.

Why should you cook at home when there are eager restaurant owners vying to cook for you? I like to be waited on hand and foot, pampered, fawned over, and entertained as much as anyone else, but my inner goddess of gluttony usually takes over and orders like Polly Pig Out at a Texas BBQ whenever I eat out. Enter restaurant pounds. Research consistently shows that when we eat out, we take in more calories than we would at comparable meals consumed in the home—as many as 200 to 1000 extra calories per meal! Cooking at home is the best way to control the quality and quantity of calories you're consuming.

kd@chefkathleen.com

SUBJECT: BORED BY MY OWN COOKING

FROM: Sharon
TO: kd@chefkathleen.com

Dear Kathleen,
I don't mind cooking, but I get bored easily.
  Sharon

REPLY: CREATE A STORAGE BANK

Dear Sharon,
Me too.
   Look for recipes when you don't need to get dinner on the table. Save your favorites in a folder. Organize them by special occasion and speedy suppers. When it's time to think about next week's menu, cook from the recipes you chose. Your shopping list will be easier to draft too. When I have a list, I'm able to buy what I truly need as opposed to stuff that looks good. Planning ahead saves time and money.
   Happy cooking, Sharon.
   Kathleen

FOOD Restaurants are known for their fancy preparations. Their big secret? Keep things simple. **Whip up a shrimp and goat cheese omelet for supper tonight.** Serve it with a salad and a glass of wine, and you can be enjoying your sweetie's company before the sun goes down. Add precooked and diced shrimp, chopped fresh basil, mint, and parsley, and a tiny bit of goat cheese to scrambled egg whites and cook omelet- or frittata-style.

FUN **Time for a cookbook splurge.** You can't have too many in your lifetime, that's for sure. And I don't always go to the bookstore to stock up; there are a lot of great finds at library sales and garage sales, but get there early!

FITNESS If you're going to eat out, build exercise into the experience. Walk to and from the restaurant. If that's not possible, take a walk before or after dinner. Keep it fun: walk near a restaurant or at a park along the way. **You will consume more calories when you eat out.** You need to work them off if you don't want to wear them.

FOCUS If you're feeling helpless and hopeless, turn it around. You have the power to take control of your life. Cooking is easy and can be a lot of fun once you get the hang of It. **Cooking will help you lose weight and keep it off.** You will feel more in control. You can go to bed every night knowing you did your very best by your self and your family.

Homework Assignment

It's my theory that most people hate to cook for one of three reasons: their kitchens look like *Sanford and Son's* last haul, the most time they've spent in their kitchens is the time it takes to pass through them, or they suffer from low culinary self-esteem.

Figure out what it is that's keeping you out of the kitchen. Make a list of the reasons. Now give the list to someone you love and trust to help you come up with solutions. Be open-minded. Take the list and suggestions to heart. Make up your mind that you are going to cook at home more than you eat out.

YOUR GAME PLAN (STATE YOUR FOOD AND EXERCISE GOALS FOR THE WEEK)

Potato Seafood Chowder

SERVES 4 *Fish is an essential ingredient for heart health. You might start out by serving some of the leaner fishes, such as cod and snapper. I haven't cut the creaminess and hearty texture one expects in a bowlful of chowder, but I have cut out the cream.*

2 ounces pancetta or country bacon, cut into ½-inch slices

1 medium onion, finely diced

1 cup diced celery

2 tennis ball–size Yukon Gold potatoes, about ½ pound, peeled and cut into ¼-inch dice

½ pound green beans, trimmed, cut into bite-size pieces

1 cup fresh corn kernels (about 2 ears)

2 cups low-sodium chicken broth or clam juice

2 sprigs fresh rosemary

1 bay leaf

¾ pound cod, cut into bite-size chunks

1 cup fat-free milk or evaporated milk

PLACE pancetta in a medium saucepan over medium-high heat and cook for about 1 minute, uncovered. Add onion and celery and cook for 5 to 6 minutes, or until onion has completely softened.

ADD potatoes, green beans, and corn and cook for 3 minutes. Add broth, rosemary, and bay leaf. Bring to a boil, then reduce to a simmer and cook for about 10 minutes. Add fish, cover, and cook for 10 minutes. Add milk and cook until soup is warm, about 5 minutes. Remove bay leaf and serve.

■ *You can substitute thyme for the rosemary.*

WHAT'S PANCETTA?

Pancetta, often called Italian bacon, is widely available in gourmet grocery stores and Italian delis. Bacon is made from brined pork sides and pork belly that has been cured and smoked. Pancetta is made from just the belly and is salt-cured and dried for several months but not smoked. You can buy it sliced or in a chunk. Calorie for calorie, bacon and pancetta are neck and neck and should be consumed in small quantities on special occasions. Using a small amount to flavor an entire batch of soup or stew is a great way to reap the flavor rewards without the calorie consequences.

What I ate:

What I wish I hadn't:

What I did for exercise:

Tuesday

What I ate:

What I wish I hadn't:

What I did for exercise:

Wednesday

What I ate:

What I wish I hadn't:

What I did for exercise:

Thursday

What I ate:

What I wish I hadn't:

What I did for exercise:

Friday

What I ate:

What I wish I hadn't:

What I did for exercise:

REPORT CARD

I REALLY FELT GREAT WHEN I

I CAN GET BETTER AT

NEW FOODS I'M GOING TO TRY

NEXT WEEK I'M GOING TO

GIVE YOURSELF A GRADE
FOR THIS WEEK'S EFFORTS:

Saturday

What I ate:

What I wish I hadn't:

What I did for exercise:

Sunday

What I ate:

What I wish I hadn't:

What I did for exercise:

Suffering from 5:00 PMS? You avoid thinking about dinner until the clock strikes 5:00 P.M., at which time you get stuck in traffic on your way to an overcrowded grocery store. You unload the groceries, troubleshoot through after-school minutiae, and attempt to cook something your family will eat. All this just in time to do the dishes, finish up the homework, settle six fights, throw in a load of laundry, read bedtime stories, and collapse. It's no wonder you're cranky.

kd@chefkathleen.com

SUBJECT: FORAGING FOR TROUBLE

FROM: Stephanie
TO: kd@chefkathleen.com

Dear Kathleen,
I'm a busy mom. After I've picked the kids up from school, I'm usually really tired and I start snacking. I overeat at dinner and wind up the evening with a glass of wine as I look for something sweet. I wake up the next morning feeling bad about my lack of self-control. I have to get 45 pounds off!
   Stephanie

REPLY: START TOMORROW'S DINNER TONIGHT

Dear Stephanie,
If you were in a power-outage situation with no car to drive, chances are you'd be able to get something on the table. Work with what you have and do your best to stay one day ahead. Plan tomorrow's dinner tonight. It will focus you. My grandmother used to half cook the next night's meal before she cleaned up the kitchen every evening. When she arrived home from her commute, she had little more to do than reheat the meal. Keep your pantry extremely well stocked and be on the lookout for easy recipes you can toss together and eat. Pre-portion all of the high-calorie elements of dinner. No family-style anything, except salad and veggies healthfully prepared. Out of sight, out of mind, out of mouth.
   Kathleen

FOOD **Ask everyone you know for a favorite emergency meal.** To start, you're looking for five that you can get on the table in your sleep. Write down all those that appeal to you. One of my favorites is nonstick-pan-"fried" cube steaks, microwaved green beans or broccoli, and tossed salad.

FUN **Grab a pad of paper and a pencil and go to the bookstore with the absolute best inventory of magazines.** Sit on the floor and look through any with recipes. You don't have to *buy* all or any of them. Leafing through them will inspire you to cook, you'll walk away having learned a few techniques, and if you find a recipe or two short enough, jot them down. They have to be easy!

FITNESS Pop Quiz. **Are you working to your true fitness potential?** If not, why not? Evaluate tomorrow's workout, think about how you can get and keep your heart rate up past too-breathless-to-chat-now for twenty to thirty minutes and just do it!

FOCUS You're eighteen weeks into transforming your eating and exercise habits. **How far have you come?** How far do you want to go? Think about it.

Homework Assignment
Pantry check: Is there anything in there you can turn into supper? If not, why not? Put an enormous amount of effort into cleaning out and restocking your pantry. If you don't have the basics on hand, how on earth can you get dinner on the table in a hurry? Your new list of pantry basics will include the ingredients in the emergency suppers you research and nail down this week.

YOUR GAME PLAN (STATE YOUR FOOD AND EXERCISE GOALS FOR THE WEEK)

Spicy Chicken Meatballs

SERVES 6 TO 8 *One cannot expect to achieve inner peace living a life devoid of meatballs, unless of course you're a vegetarian, which I am not.*

FOR THE SAUCE
- 1 small onion, finely diced
- 1 garlic clove, minced
- 1 28-ounce can ground peeled tomatoes
- 1 teaspoon dried thyme (or 2 teaspoons chopped fresh)
- 1 teaspoon dried oregano
  Coarse salt and cracked black pepper

FOR THE MEATBALLS
- 1 pound ground white-meat chicken (see next page)
- 2 cups fresh bread crumbs
- 1 egg white
- 1 garlic clove, minced
- 1/2 cup loosely packed grated Parmesan cheese
- 1/4 cup loosely packed, finely chopped fresh parsley
- 1/2 teaspoon dried thyme (or 1 teaspoon chopped fresh)
- 1/4 teaspoon cayenne pepper

SAUCE: Place onion in a medium saucepan with 1/4 cup water. Turn heat to medium and cook until completely softened, 5 to 10 minutes. Add garlic, tomatoes, thyme, and oregano. Stir until combined. Bring to a boil, then reduce to a simmer. Taste and adjust seasonings with salt and pepper. Cook until slightly thickened, 8 to 10 minutes.

MEATBALLS: Preheat oven to 350°F. Place chicken in a large bowl. Add bread crumbs, egg white, garlic, Parmesan cheese, parsley, thyme, and cayenne. Mix until completely combined and form into fifty 1-inch meatballs.

POUR sauce into a baking dish, place formed meatballs in sauce, and bake, uncovered, until cooked through and golden, 15 to 20 minutes.

WHAT GOES AROUND COMES AROUND

Just because the label says ground turkey or ground chicken doesn't mean it's lean or low-calorie. Skin, fat, and dark meat are often ground in with white-meat parts. With an eye for calorie and fat counts, read labels and compare the serving size you're likely to consume versus the one listed on the package. If there's no label on the product, ring the bell, hand the butcher a package of white-meat chicken or turkey breasts, and politely ask him or her to grind it for you on the spot. Or do it yourself: place 1-inch cubes of white-meat chicken or turkey in a food processor and pulse. The meat will be more juicy if you don't grind it too finely.

Monday

What I ate:

What I wish I hadn't:

What I did for exercise:

Tuesday

What I ate:

What I wish I hadn't:

What I did for exercise:

Wednesday

What I ate:

What I wish I hadn't:

What I did for exercise:

Thursday

What I ate:

What I wish I hadn't:

What I did for exercise:

Friday

What I ate:

What I wish I hadn't:

What I did for exercise:

REPORT CARD

Saturday

I REALLY FELT GREAT WHEN I

I CAN GET BETTER AT

NEW FOODS I'M GOING TO TRY

NEXT WEEK I'M GOING TO

GIVE YOURSELF A GRADE
FOR THIS WEEK'S EFFORTS:

What I ate:

What I wish I hadn't:

What I did for exercise:

Sunday

What I ate:

What I wish I hadn't:

What I did for exercise:

Working toward your ideal self and ideal behaviors begins with embracing what you're realistically capable of achieving. Focusing on achieving my body's ideal weight, the weight at which it functions the very best, is a goal that feels right. When I measure myself against unrealistic standards, my voice of self-loathing launches into why-me rants. Don't go there.

kd@chefkathleen.com

SUBJECT: I THINK I CAN'T
FROM: Millie
TO: kd@chefkathleen.com

Dear Kathleen,
I've been dieting my whole life. I'm still fat. I hate how I look. When I'm really upset, I eat out of control, and I don't know how to stop. I really don't believe that I'll ever lose the weight.
  Millie

REPLY: THINK YOU CAN AND
         GET A PLAN!

Dear Millie,
I asked Dr. Dale Atkins, Ph.D., a psychologist and author, to read your letter and respond: "Begin to act as a person who has the ability to eat healthfully and comfortably, who can make choices, feel good about food, and appreciate its positive value. Visualizing this ideal self will help you move closer to that image. We do better when we examine our behavior and stay away from such damaging self talk as 'I'm such an out-of-control pig' and 'I've never been successful before.'

  "I worked with a young woman who'd go into the kitchen and eat a box or more of cereal after everyone went to bed. To break herself of this habit, she learned to ask herself, 'What would my ideal self do?' Over time, she was able to take control."

  Think and have a plan, Millie, and like the Little Engine that did, you can too!
  Kathleen

FOOD If there's nothing in the house for Beatrice, Baroness of Bad Behavior, to eat, she can't stuff her frustration with food. **Challenge yourself to stock your fridge with low-calorie, superhealthy snacks.** Place them at eye level so when you whip open that fridge door in a frustrated feeding frenzy, there's something safe for you to eat. One of my all-time favorite treats is a half papaya topped with strawberry yogurt and sliced bananas. It's a decadent splurge that takes no time to prepare.

FUN When you have some time, go into the kitchen and cook something healthy. **Make one of those recipes that sound great but that you normally skip over because you're too busy.** The feeling of accomplishment and satisfaction that comes when you're tucking that good-for-your-body meal onto your refrigerator shelf is truly liberating.

FITNESS When I'm stressed to the gills, I don't *feel* like exercising. I *feel* like eating. **I've learned to stop and evaluate how exercising will make me feel versus consuming unplanned calories.** Sometimes I'm in an emotional stupor as I reach for my bike shoes and fill up my water bottles, but I go through the motions. I don't try to force a normal workout. But the minute I'm on that bike, the feelings of accomplishment for having gotten there fuel me as nothing else can. I've had some of my best rides in my "darkest" hours.

FOCUS You have the ability to change your behavior patterns. Believe that you can, access the kind of help you need, access support along the way, and you will achieve absolutely everything you set your mind to.

Homework Assignment Practice becoming conscious of your eating patterns. Take note of when you're eating for hunger and when you're eating out of stress or boredom. Tune in to how you're feeling. Get out a pad of paper and a pencil, or sit down at your computer and vent. Write freely. It's impossible to change habits that aren't serving you if you're not fully aware of how, when, and why they strike.

YOUR GAME PLAN (STATE YOUR FOOD AND EXERCISE GOALS FOR THE WEEK)

Grilled Beef and Chopped Vegetable Salad

SERVES 6 *I call this refrigerator salad because I make some version of it every time I have a refrigerator full of veggies. It doesn't really matter what you put into it. The dressing is the important part.*

¼ cup red wine vinegar

1½ tablespoons fresh lemon juice

1 teaspoon grated lemon zest

½ teaspoon sugar

   Coarse salt

1 tablespoon capers, rinsed and chopped

1 tablespoon Dijon mustard

2 tablespoons honey mustard

2 teaspoons olive oil

   Cracked black pepper

   Olive oil spray

¾ pound boneless flank steak

1 bunch asparagus, ends trimmed

2 ears corn, husked

1 green zucchini, quartered lengthwise

1 pint cherry tomatoes, cut in half

8 cups washed torn garden lettuces

½ cup loosely packed, coarsely chopped fresh basil

FIRE up your outdoor grill. Meanwhile, in a large salad bowl that you'll serve the salad in, whisk together vinegar, lemon juice, and lemon zest. Add sugar and a pinch of salt. Stir until dissolved. Add capers, Dijon mustard, honey mustard, olive oil, and black pepper to taste. Set aside.

SPRAY meat, asparagus, corn, and zucchini with a thin coating of olive oil and sprinkle with salt and pepper. Arrange on grill. Remove veggies and meat when done to your liking. Transfer meat to a cutting board to rest.

CUT corn kernels off cob directly into salad bowl. Chop asparagus and zucchini and add to salad bowl. Add cherry tomatoes. Add salad greens and basil. Toss to coat well. Divide among serving plates.

THINLY slice steak and distribute evenly among salads. Serve.

■ *To make this recipe indoors, spread the veggies on rimmed cookie sheets and roast them.*

10 GREAT SNACKS

1. A baked sweet potato with low-fat yogurt, chopped fresh cilantro, and a squeeze of lime

2. A bowl of oatmeal with fruit

3. A microwave-cooked spaghetti squash with marinara sauce, chopped fresh basil, and grated Parmesan cheese

4. A plate of warm lentils with a squeeze of fresh lemon and a dollop of Greek-style yogurt

5. A strawberry banana smoothie: Blend 1 cup strawberries, half a frozen banana, ½ cup skim or soy milk, and ice

6. A heaping helping of steamed or microwave-cooked broccoli tossed with salad dressing

7. Ripe watermelon chunks

8. A slice of toasted whole-grain bread spread with a little peanut butter and a dollop of all-fruit jam

9. Microwave-cooked green beans tossed with a drizzle of olive oil, a squeeze of lemon, and a few shavings of Parmesan

10. A baked potato topped with something good for you

Monday

What I ate:

What I wish I hadn't:

What I did for exercise:

Tuesday

What I ate:

What I wish I hadn't:

What I did for exercise:

Wednesday

What I ate:

What I wish I hadn't:

What I did for exercise:

Thursday

What I ate:

What I wish I hadn't:

What I did for exercise:

Friday

What I ate:

What I wish I hadn't:

What I did for exercise:

I REALLY FELT GREAT WHEN I

I CAN GET BETTER AT

NEW FOODS I'M GOING TO TRY

NEXT WEEK I'M GOING TO

GIVE YOURSELF A GRADE
FOR THIS WEEK'S EFFORTS:

Saturday

What I ate:

What I wish I hadn't:

What I did for exercise:

Sunday

What I ate:

What I wish I hadn't:

What I did for exercise:

Grocery-store road rules are few, plain, and simple. Shop the outer aisles. Don't shop hungry. If it's not on your list, it doesn't go in your cart. If it's in a box, and it's not baking soda, chances are it probably won't serve you nutritionally. Start in the produce section and fill up your cart. Cruise over to the dairy, meat, and fish areas. Hit the cereal aisle, whip through the section with legumes, whole grains, and whole-grain breads, and then hightail it out of there. Steer clear of the freezer section unless you've got frozen fruit on your list. Ben & Jerry and all their cousins are there. That kind of family reunion you don't need.

kd@chefkathleen.com

SUBJECT: THE DEVIL MADE ME BUY IT

FROM: Regina
TO: kd@chefkathleen.com

Dear Kathleen,
I love grocery shopping and I love trying all the new products. I bring home stuff I know I shouldn't be eating. Any tips?
  Regina

REPLY: DELIVER YOURSELF FROM TEMPTATION

Dear Regina,
For me, shopping in a well-stocked grocery store can be like asking a heroin addict to shop at the all-night drug mart with a gift card. That's why I usually shop at a specialty produce market that carries most of what I need and doesn't have giant cookie displays or freezers full of gourmet ice cream I can't resist. Impulse buying leads to impulse consumption. If you need to shop at supermarkets but face the same challenges I do, shop with a friend or a child you want to teach healthy habits to.
  Kathleen

FOOD **Invite your ideal self to dinner every night this week.** Think fit, fast meals: grilled fish with diced avocados and halved cherry tomatoes tossed with chopped fresh cilantro, grated jalapeño, lime, and salt — with a giant salad on the side. For dessert? A quarter cup each of raspberry and mango sorbet, topped with blueberries and a sprinkling of granola.

FUN Go to a farmers' market, a fruit stand, or a produce market every single week for the rest of the summer and the rest of your life if you're lucky enough to have access to one or all three year-round. **There's nothing like fresh-from-the-earth, just-picked produce to inspire you to cook and eat healthy.**

FITNESS In December 2001, the U.S. surgeon general, Dr. David Satcher, issued a recommendation to add about thirty minutes of moderate-intensity activity each day to your customary daily activities. **Strive to take about 10,000 steps a day and you *will* improve your health.**

FOCUS Get a pedometer and see how many steps you're averaging daily. **Challenge yourself to increase the number of steps you take each day.** You can get a decent pedometer for less than $30 in any sporting goods department. If you're currently logging about 2400 and aim for 10,000 and achieve 3000 steps, you've already made huge strides!

Homework Assignment Ready, set, shop! Cooking at home efficiently begins with a meticulously thought-out plan. If you have a tendency to take everyone's thoughts and feelings into consideration, get over it. You don't have time. When you're the chief bottle washer and cook, you get to pick the menus, and you must.

Gather seven recipes lickety-split and make a list of all the ingredients. Then whip out a pen and paper and draft your grocery list by aisle. The first item on the list should be just inside the front door. The last items should be closest to the checkout so you can get in and out of there quickly. Make sure you eat before you go.

YOUR GAME PLAN (STATE YOUR FOOD AND EXERCISE GOALS FOR THE WEEK)

Chickpea, Cucumber, and Apple Salad

SERVES 6 TO 8 *This unlikely combination is out-of-this-world great, especially when you're craving an instant-gratification, high-protein lunch or light supper.*

¼ **cup orange juice**

2 **tablespoons red wine vinegar**

1 **tablespoon olive oil**

2 **teaspoons honey**

½ **cup loosely packed, coarsely chopped fresh mint**

Coarse salt and cracked black pepper

1 **15-ounce can chickpeas, rinsed and drained**

1 **large cucumber, peeled, seeded, and very thinly sliced**

4 **large ribs celery, very thinly sliced**

1 **small fennel, cored and very thinly sliced**

1 **apple, cored, cut in half lengthwise, and very thinly sliced**

1 **head butter lettuce, torn**

IN a large salad bowl, whisk together orange juice, vinegar, oil, and honey. Stir in mint. Add salt and pepper to taste.

ADD chickpeas, cucumber, celery, fennel, and apple. Gently toss until combined. Taste and adjust seasonings. Serve on lettuce.

YOU SAY ANISE, I SAY FENNEL

No matter what the sign says, fennel is heavenly delicious. It's got a celery-like crunch. Once cored, it's just as easy to slice as celery. Though the stalks and feathery tops are good to eat, this vegetable is prized for its edible, aromatic, mild licorice-flavored bulb. It's delicious eaten raw in salads, stewed in soups, braised, grilled, or roasted. It pairs particularly well with oranges, olives, lemon, cucumber, apples, delicate leafy greens, and Parmesan cheese. It's wonderful with pork, chicken, and fish. You can use dried fennel seeds in many dishes, especially those that include sausages and spaghetti sauces.

Monday

What I ate:

What I wish I hadn't:

What I did for exercise:

Tuesday

What I ate:

What I wish I hadn't:

What I did for exercise:

Wednesday

What I ate:

What I wish I hadn't:

What I did for exercise:

Thursday

What I ate:

What I wish I hadn't:

What I did for exercise:

Friday

What I ate:

What I wish I hadn't:

What I did for exercise:

REPORT CARD

I REALLY FELT GREAT WHEN I

What I ate:

I CAN GET BETTER AT

What I wish I hadn't:

What I did for exercise:

NEW FOODS I'M GOING TO TRY

What I ate:

NEXT WEEK I'M GOING TO

What I wish I hadn't:

What I did for exercise:

GIVE YOURSELF A GRADE
FOR THIS WEEK'S EFFORTS:

WEEK
20

Lance Armstrong didn't win the Tour de France seven years in a row by himself. He had a team—cyclists he rides with out on the road—a team of professionals that manage them, and he had a home team, his family and friends. If you've never considered that losing weight and keeping it off requires a team, consider it now. Why shouldn't you take advantage of every single resource available to you to reach your goals?

kd@chefkathleen.com

SUBJECT: LONE RANGER
FROM: Lissa
TO: kd@chefkathleen.com

Dear Kathleen,
My husband and I both could stand to lose about 50 pounds, but he'll have no part of eating healthy. How can I get him to come around?
Lissa

REPLY: COP A 'TUDE

Dear Lissa,
I posed your query to the forum at chefkathleen.com. Here's what weight-loss success story Stephanie had to say about getting her husband on board: "I find that my attitude makes a huge difference in the things my husband will try. By projecting that I'm not cooking diet food, that I'm merely making dinner, we end up eating a healthy, well-rounded meal, and he's none the wiser. I make it a point to always set out healthy options. If he wants to try the new veggie side dish fine; if not, I don't call attention to it. If I don't stress over it, no one else will either. Most of the time my husband will gladly try a spoonful of whatever I make, no matter how foreign it may seem to him. And, fortunately, most of the time he'll eat it. He and I are both learning to eat new foods. Sometimes he says, 'It's not my favorite,' but that's OK. It's still a huge victory to me when he tries something new."
Kathleen

FOOD Lance's coach, Chris Carmichael, counsels him on nutrition. **If you're strapped for cash, a couple of Saturday garage sales will yield enough money for a trip to a nutritionist.** There are plenty of books to guide and inspire you, and there are free online resources. If you're looking for references, log on to the fan forums at chefkathleen.com and ask for help. I'm there every single day. Utilize the professionals on the site, brainstorm, and troubleshoot with the enthusiastic fans.

FUN **Read a book about someone who has overcome great odds.** *It's Not About the Bike: My Journey Back to Life,* by Lance Armstrong with Sally Jenkins, is the story of Armstrong's triumph over adversity. You don't have to be a fan of cycling to appreciate the lessons he imparts in this book. They're yours for the taking. Don't waste them.

FITNESS Every day this week, apply to your own workout routine a key principle that one of your role models practices daily. Think about his discipline, commitment, and work ethic. **Let him inspire you to take yourself to another level.**

FOCUS In an interview on the Saturday before he rolled into Paris to claim his seventh straight tour victory, Armstrong explained his success. "It's a full-year commitment. That's the secret. **The answer is total, full commitment and hard work.**"

Homework Assignment Who's on your team? Get out a pad of paper and pencil. Make columns for "Food," "Fitness," "Medical," and "Psychological Resources." Under "Food," you might put your spouse or your kids or the name of a Web site such as fitday.com to help you calculate and track calories. Under "Psychological Resources," you might have the name of a health professional, a support group, or some helpful books you've read lately. Are there enough team members? You don't have to do this alone. Enlist the help you deserve. Achieve the results you want.

YOUR GAME PLAN (STATE YOUR FOOD AND EXERCISE GOALS FOR THE WEEK)

Chicken and Wild Rice One-Pan Supper

SERVES 4 TO 6 *If you're trying to get fit and healthy and also work in more servings of whole grains, this recipe is a delicious way to do it.*

2 teaspoons olive oil

1 medium onion, cut into ½-inch dice

3 garlic cloves, very thinly sliced

½ cup black or green olives, drained, pitted, and chopped

1 28-ounce can diced tomatoes

¾ cup low-sodium chicken broth

2 tablespoons tomato paste

1 teaspoon dried thyme

1 teaspoon dried oregano

½ teaspoon cayenne pepper

1 bay leaf

1 cup wild rice, rinsed well and drained

1 pound boneless, skinless chicken breast, cut into 1-inch pieces

Coarse salt and cracked black pepper

HEAT oil over medium-high heat in a large pot until hot but not smoking. Add onion, garlic, and 2 tablespoons water. Cover and cook until onion has completely softened, about 10 minutes.

ADD remaining ingredients. Bring to a boil, reduce to a simmer, and cook, covered, for 45 to 55 minutes, or until rice has absorbed most of the liquid and is cooked through. Season with salt and pepper to taste. Turn off heat and let stand 10 minutes, covered. Remove bay leaf. Serve.

Monday

What I ate:

What I wish I hadn't:

What I did for exercise:

Tuesday

What I ate:

What I wish I hadn't:

What I did for exercise:

Wednesday

What I ate:

What I wish I hadn't:

What I did for exercise:

Thursday

What I ate:

What I wish I hadn't:

What I did for exercise:

Friday

What I ate:

What I wish I hadn't:

What I did for exercise:

Saturday

I REALLY FELT GREAT WHEN I

What I ate:

What I wish I hadn't:

I CAN GET BETTER AT

What I did for exercise:

Sunday

NEW FOODS I'M GOING TO TRY

What I ate:

What I wish I hadn't:

NEXT WEEK I'M GOING TO

What I did for exercise:

GIVE YOURSELF A GRADE
FOR THIS WEEK'S EFFORTS:

Environmental control is paramount to your success. If you've got cake bombs in your pantry, chocolates in your underwear drawer, and five kinds of ice cream in your freezer, half your day will be spent talking yourself in and out of consuming this stuff. Waste half your life trying to prove you can cohabitate with Ho Hos or get rid of the junk and be done with it. Conduct regular clean sweeps. The only thing that keeps me honest are routine knock-knock visits from the local division of my EPA in the form of my family and friends: "Why do you have four bars of baking chocolate, Kathleen? You don't bake."

kd@chefkathleen.com

SUBJECT: ENOUGH FOOD FOR AN ARMY

FROM: D.C.

TO: kd@chefkathleen.com

Dear Kathleen,

Mother used to keep enough food in the house to feed an army. She stockpiled food in the basement and the garage. And now I do it. I tell myself it's for emergencies and so I don't have to shop all the time, but it's driving my husband nuts.

D.C.

REPLY: RATIONS AND ESSENTIALS

Dear D.C.,

Go to the library and check out *I'm Okay, You're My Parents: How to Overcome Guilt, Let Go of Anger, and Create a Relationship That Works,* by Dr. Dale Atkins, Ph.D. Some things to think about:

Pretend the power went out. Distribute all the food to friends and neighbors before it spoils. You'll save in emotional currency tenfold what the food cost you.

Donate as much of your stash as you can part with to a local charity.

Close down sections of your "food bank" shelf by shelf.

Kathleen

FOOD Stop rationalizing the purchase of foods that tempt you to overeat. **Make your grocery list in advance and don't shop hungry.** Reward yourself every time you come home with a "clean" cartful of food. When I'm "dying" for sugar, one of my favorite treats is a Medjool date straight from the freezer. I remove the pit and replace it with a whole walnut (minus the shell, of course). It's deliciously sweet and the perfect cure for my sweet tooth.

FUN Go through your stack of unread magazines, grab an ice-cold glass of water, curl up in your favorite chair, outside if possible, and read one issue cover to cover. At the very least, pencil it in for later today. **Thirty minutes off does wonders for stress levels.**

FITNESS If your life isn't set up to accommodate your fitness goals, they'll go unmet. **What can you do to ensure that exercise becomes nonnegotiable?**

FOCUS Are you *really* hungry? I ask myself this question every single time I think I "need" something to eat and every time my stomach starts to grumble or, worse, howl. **I review what I've eaten up to that point in the day.** I quickly evaluate the stress I may be under, the amount of sleep I've had, and my goals for the rest of the day. This dialogue has helped me to keep many pounds from coming back.

Homework Assignment

Homework Assignment Open all your cupboards, the fridge, the freezer, the junk drawer, your nightstand and dresser drawers, the glove compartment, your "gym" bag, your desk drawer at work—anywhere you stash food. Pull out every single temptation. Why keep foods that lure you away from your plan, Pied Piper–style? Because you feel as if you should be more in control? Removing temptations *is* taking control. Give yourself every competitive edge and you *will* win.

YOUR GAME PLAN (STATE YOUR FOOD AND EXERCISE GOALS FOR THE WEEK)

Pork Chops and Citrus Rice with Prunes and Apricots

SERVES 4 *This is an easy one-dish dinner that you can get on the table with relative ease.*

If you have a skillet with tall sides and a tight-fitting lid, you can make this recipe in one dish all at one time. If not, you might want to fry the pork chops in a nonstick pan and cook the rice in a 2-quart saucepan.

2 teaspoons olive oil
1 pound pork chops (4 thin-cut)
2 cups chicken broth
1 tablespoon grated orange zest
1 cup fresh orange juice
2 cups instant brown rice
4 scallions, white and green parts, minced
½ cup chopped pitted prunes
½ cup chopped dried apricots
1 tablespoon chopped fresh sage

HEAT oil in a large skillet (see above) until hot but not smoking. Add pork chops and cook until golden brown, turning once, about 5 minutes.

ADD remaining ingredients. Bring to a boil, reduce to a simmer, cover, and cook for 5 minutes. Turn off heat and let stand, covered, for 5 minutes more. Serve.

■ *If you can't find instant brown rice, substitute 1 cup regular brown rice and soak for 1 hour before cooking. Cook according to package instructions until tender. Add cooked rice to skillet in place of instant rice.*

Monday

What I ate:

What I wish I hadn't:

What I did for exercise:

Tuesday

What I ate:

What I wish I hadn't:

What I did for exercise:

Wednesday

What I ate:

What I wish I hadn't:

What I did for exercise:

Thursday

What I ate:

What I wish I hadn't:

What I did for exercise:

Friday

What I ate:

What I wish I hadn't:

What I did for exercise:

Saturday

I REALLY FELT GREAT WHEN I

What I ate:

What I wish I hadn't:

I CAN GET BETTER AT

What I did for exercise:

Sunday

NEW FOODS I'M GOING TO TRY

What I ate:

What I wish I hadn't:

NEXT WEEK I'M GOING TO

What I did for exercise:

GIVE YOURSELF A GRADE
FOR THIS WEEK'S EFFORTS:

I've said it all. I've heard it all: "I'm going to throw out all my junk food, eat only salad, and exercise six days a week." All-or-nothing thinking is sink, not swim, counter-productive behavior that will never lead you to the success you're capable of achieving. How much time are *you* willing to waste?

kd@chefkathleen.com

SUBJECT: MY STARTING-TOMORROW DIET FAILED

FROM: Sophie
TO: kd@chefkathleen.com

Dear Kathleen,
I've been "starting tomorrow" for five years. I'm miserable with how I look and feel and with how much I weigh. How do I stop starting over and how can I stay motivated?
Sophie

REPLY: PITY PARTY RAIN CHECK

Dear Sophie,
Stop and just be. Be thankful for the gift of choice, the gift of opportunities, and the gift of possibilities before you. Be thankful for a clear, thinking mind, food on the table, and an able body. Be purposeful, be determined, be relentless, be faithful to the body you have and the health you've been given. Be active, be humble, be patient, be kind, be still. Believe.

I asked weight-loss success story Kendra how she stays motivated. "Find something other than food that motivates you. Reward yourself, not just for weight loss, but also for positive behavior. I love beautiful flowers, especially roses, so I stopped by a flower market close to home every time I lost 10 pounds. It got so that whenever I brought flowers in to work, my coworkers knew I'd hit another milestone and cheered me on. Sometimes they would surprise me with flowers. Talk about motivation."
Kathleen

FOOD No-nonsense advice from weight-loss success story Dawn: "Eliminate all-or-nothing behavior: 'I ate two cookies, so I might as well finish the package.' Instead, throw the cookies into your neighbor's trash can. **Teach yourself to get back on track at the very next meal.**" My all-or-nothing diet included polishing off pints of ice cream in a single sitting. Now when I'm craving ice cream and have no calories to spend, I whip up thick smoothies. Chocolate-flavored light soy milk, half a frozen banana, water, lots of ice, and a tablespoon each of unsweetened cocoa powder, nonfat dry milk, oatmeal, and wheat bran whipped to frosty perfection is a midsummer night's dream.

FUN **Identify the hardest, most unrealistic restriction you've placed on yourself.** "I'm cutting out dairy and sugar." Write it down on a sheet of paper and shred it to pieces. Doesn't that feel better?

FITNESS Dawn says, "When I scaled my exercise time commitment and expectations down to twenty or twenty-five minutes, I actually started exercising on a regular basis. **I exercise more now because I don't quit and give up anymore.**"

FOCUS Think back to a particularly long and challenging skill you've mastered: learning to play a musical instrument, earning a degree, painting the house, or raising a child—you couldn't quit in the middle. You set out to accomplish something and you did. You probably thought about the route in advance, refueled along the way, and somehow found the inner strength to forge ahead when you felt like quitting. **The act of losing weight and achieving your health goals is just another journey.** You've already proven that you have what it takes to make it.

Homework Assignment Make a list of some of the extreme goals in eating and exercise that you've set for yourself. Next to each item, write down more realistic ones. Finally, write down how you can baby-step your way toward realistic behavior. Change "I will exercise six or seven times a week" to "I will be physically active five times a week. I will take leisurely walks on days I'm not up to my full routine."

YOUR GAME PLAN (STATE YOUR FOOD AND EXERCISE GOALS FOR THE WEEK)

Mostly Whole-Wheat Pizza Dough

SERVES 6 TO 8 *Makes 2 thick-crust 10-inch pizzas or 4 thin-crust 8-inch pizzas. This dough keeps well in the refrigerator overnight or in the freezer for about 6 months. Place a bag of the frozen dough on the counter before you leave for work. By the time you cruise in, the dough will be ready to roll, top, and bake. Use it to make the Gourmet Asparagus, Prosciutto, and Provolone Pizza in Week 25 or top with your own favorite low-fat combinations.*

2½ **cups whole-wheat flour**
1 **cup unbleached all-purpose flour, plus more as needed**
2 **packages active dry yeast**
1 **teaspoon salt**
½ **teaspoon sugar**
½ **teaspoon olive oil for bowl**
Cornmeal for sprinkling

PLACE flours, yeast, salt, and sugar in a food processor and pulse to blend. Pour 1½ cups water through feed tube with motor running. Process until dough forms a ball. Place in an oiled bowl and cover with plastic wrap. Let rise in warm spot until doubled in bulk, about 2 hours.

PREHEAT oven to highest setting. Punch down dough and cut in half. Place one half of dough on a generously floured work surface. Form loosely into a ball and stretch into a circle. Using a floured rolling pin, roll into a large, thin circle. Sprinkle a rimless cookie sheet generously with cornmeal, transfer dough to sheet, and add toppings.

PUT cookie sheet with pizza on bottom rack of oven. Bake for 10 to 12 minutes, or until golden. Roll out remaining dough and add desired toppings and bake or freeze dough in freezer bags.

TRUE OR FALSE?

A slice of carry-out pizza can have more calories than a fast-food deluxe burger. True or false? And you usually have two to three slices of pizza? If you answered True, you've got two good reasons to make your own pizza at home. It's a great way to get the family together, topping their own mini pizzas, and, more importantly, controlling the quantity and quality of the ingredients. Pizza doesn't have to cost you a half day's worth of calories and a whole day's worth of saturated fat and sodium. Make your own and have a ball!

What I ate:

What I wish I hadn't:

What I did for exercise:

Tuesday

What I ate:

What I wish I hadn't:

What I did for exercise:

Wednesday

What I ate:

_____

What I wish I hadn't:

_____

What I did for exercise:

Thursday

What I ate:

_____

What I wish I hadn't:

_____

What I did for exercise:

Friday

What I ate:

_____

What I wish I hadn't:

_____

What I did for exercise:

REPORT CARD

I REALLY FELT GREAT WHEN I

I CAN GET BETTER AT

NEW FOODS I'M GOING TO TRY

NEXT WEEK I'M GOING TO

GIVE YOURSELF A GRADE
FOR THIS WEEK'S EFFORTS:

Saturday

What I ate:

What I wish I hadn't:

What I did for exercise:

Sunday

What I ate:

What I wish I hadn't:

What I did for exercise:

According to a survey by the California Table Grapes Commission, 92 percent of Americans snack. According to the commission, on average, men get in just one serving a day of fruits and vegetables, while women get just two. The most consumed vegetable? French fries!

Instead of always focusing on the foods you shouldn't be eating, start fantasizing about all the foods you *can* eat. What could be finer than sharing watermelon slices with family and friends on a hot July day? Or devouring slices of ripe mango on a dreary winter morning? Splurge on fruit. Save money on laundry soap, but don't bypass the produce aisle.

SUGAR SOLUTION

Every time I go for a long walk or a bike ride, I come home "starving" for sugar. Determined to break the crave-sugar, eat-sugar cycle, one night I pulled a pint of blueberries out of the fridge and had a few. I munched on them while I prepared my supper. It was bachelorette night: a microwave-baked sweet potato with low-fat plain yogurt, which I prepared first. I ate it while I cooked my next course: microwaved broccoli with lemon and olive oil, which I ate while I reheated some leftover brown rice. Disgustingly healthy, but a restorative, filling meal. Eating in stages, especially if you're not entertaining, is a great way to feed your "need" for instant gratification when you're really hungry.

FOOD **Challenge yourself to work fruit into every meal and snack you can.** Fruit with your cold cereal or hot oatmeal, apple slices spread with peanut butter midmorning, mango on your salad at lunch, a pear and a slice of cheese midafternoon, strawberries for dessert.

FUN Buy forbidden fruit, especially if you're not getting in all your servings. **The next time you shop, splurge on a variety of fruit you lust after but never buy because it's too expensive.** Buy a pint of blackberries, pineapple that's already been skinned for you, or a fruit salad that's way too much money per pound.

FITNESS Review your fitness goals. What do you *mean* you don't have any! It was your homework assignment for Week 2. It's never too late to start or start again. **Write down what you'd ultimately like to achieve fitnesswise.** Read it every morning. Next, ask yourself if your exercise plans for the day will help you reach your goal safely, effectively, and in a timely manner. If not, why not?

FOCUS Feeling overwhelmed? You can work in a whole day's worth of fruit in just one smoothie. Smoothies take just a minute or two to make and are easy to enjoy on the fly. The trick to keeping them milk-shake thick? Frozen fruit, especially bananas. When fruit passes its fruit-bowl prime, peel and trim, cut into chunks, and toss into a freezer bag. **When you don't have "time" for breakfast, blend a cup of frozen fruit with skim or soy milk or a combination of half juice and half water.** When you want to stay out of ice cream jail, smoothies are a good stand-in.

Homework Assignment Figure out how many servings of fruit you're getting in daily and commit to making up the difference. Mother Nature is a genius at portion control, packaging some fruits in single-serving sizes. A large apple, orange, peach, pear, or nectarine (tennis-ball size) constitutes a serving. Medium pieces of fruit (giant jaw-breaker size) can be eaten in pairs—two pieces per serving. With large fruits such as pineapples and melons, a thick slice is a serving.

YOUR GAME PLAN (STATE YOUR FOOD AND EXERCISE GOALS FOR THE WEEK)

Hoisin Ginger Shrimp over Brown Rice

SERVES 4 *There's no need to mince the garlic and ginger by hand if you've got a microplane grater, available at houseware and kitchen stores for about twelve bucks.*

- 1 **cup brown rice**
- ¼ **cup orange juice**
- 3 **tablespoons hoisin sauce**
- 1 **tablespoon rice wine vinegar**
- 1 **garlic clove, minced**
- 2 **tablespoons grated ginger**
- 1 **teaspoon ground cumin**
- ¼ **teaspoon red pepper flakes**
- 1½ **pounds peeled, deveined shrimp**
- 2 **teaspoons sesame oil**
- ½ **cup loosely packed, coarsely chopped fresh cilantro**
- ¼ **cup scallions, white and green parts, very thinly sliced**

COOK rice in a large pot of boiling salted water until tender and cooked through, 30 to 35 minutes. Drain and pour onto a serving platter.

IN a small bowl, whisk together orange juice, hoisin sauce, rice wine vinegar, garlic, ginger, cumin, and red pepper flakes. Set aside.

HEAT oil in a large nonstick pan over medium-high heat, add shrimp, and cook, turning once, until pink and cooked through, about 2 minutes. Remove to serving platter with rice. Add hoisin mixture to pan and bring to a boil. Immediately turn off heat, stir in cilantro and scallions, pour over shrimp and rice, and serve.

■ *If you're time-starved, you can buy your shrimp already peeled and deveined. It's available defrosted at fish markets and gourmet groceries but is a little cheaper by the pound in the frozen food section.*

WHAT'S HOISIN?

Hoisin (hoy-SIHN) is a sweet and spicy, dark and rich barbecue-like sauce used in Asian cooking. It's made from fermented soybeans, garlic, vinegar, sugar, chili peppers, and spices. If you've enjoyed mu shu pork or Peking duck, you're a fan of hoisin sauce. It's widely available in the Asian section of supermarkets.

My sister whisks a teaspoon or two of hoisin into salad dressings to perk them up. Just before you serve grilled or broiled chicken, fish, steak, shrimp, or scallops, using a pastry brush, spread a thin layer of hoisin over the top. Cook for one minute more and enjoy!

Monday

What I ate:

What I wish I hadn't:

What I did for exercise:

Tuesday

What I ate:

What I wish I hadn't:

What I did for exercise:

Wednesday

What I ate:

What I wish I hadn't:

What I did for exercise:

Thursday

What I ate:

What I wish I hadn't:

What I did for exercise:

Friday

What I ate:

What I wish I hadn't:

What I did for exercise:

Saturday

I REALLY FELT GREAT WHEN I

What I ate:

What I wish I hadn't:

I CAN GET BETTER AT

What I did for exercise:

NEW FOODS I'M GOING TO TRY

Sunday

What I ate:

What I wish I hadn't:

NEXT WEEK I'M GOING TO

What I did for exercise:

GIVE YOURSELF A GRADE
FOR THIS WEEK'S EFFORTS:

Believe that and you'll make the fad diet people even richer. But you can certainly make a better life for yourself in thirty days. Imagine if you threw in an extra twenty minutes of walking several times a week. A 150-pound woman can burn 113 calories in twenty minutes of brisk walking. Do that for five days a week, and you're on track to lose up to 8 pounds a year. If you're over thirty, you need to consume 50 fewer calories per day to compensate for a slowing metabolic rate. Get moving!

kd@chefkathleen.com

SUBJECT: SERVING SIZE SYNDROME

FROM: Betsey

TO: kd@chefkathleen.com

Dear Kathleen,
I'm always getting into trouble at the table by eating too much. I know I need to cut back my portions, but it's hard to remember how much I'm allowed to eat. How do you keep it all straight?
Betsey

REPLY: HAND-SIGNAL REHAB

Dear Betsey,
One of the viewers of my show said it best. "When thinking about portion control, I like to remember to use "hand signals":

* 1 serving of meat = the size of the palm of your hand
* 1 ounce of cheese = approximately the size of your thumb
* 1 serving of starch (mashed potatoes, rice, or pasta) = approximately the size of your fist
* To determine a 100-calorie serving of fat (dollop of oil, pat of butter), make the "OK" sign with your index finger and thumb.

Cutting back on high-calorie foods is a whole lot easier when you serve all-you-can-eat portions of low-calorie foods such as steamed or blanched veggies and salads with low-calorie dressings.
Kathleen

FOOD Replace one high-calorie snack or side dish with a lower-calorie food every day.

10 Snacks under 100 Calories:

½ cup low-fat cottage cheese

20 cherries

A perfectly cooked soft-boiled egg

2 peaches

¼ cup raw old-fashioned oatmeal, cooked (turns into a huge heaping bowlful)

2 cups chopped cauliflower or halved Brussels sprouts with lemon and a drizzle of olive oil

1 cup fat-free piña colada yogurt

3 cups arugula with ¼ cup sliced celery tossed with 2 tablespoons dressing (40 calories worth) and a paper-thin shaving or two of good Parmesan

5 egg whites, scrambled with a heaping tablespoon tomato salsa

1 whole delicious papaya with a squeeze of fresh lime juice

FUN Take a one-hour me-time break today. Rest and time "away," even if it's only in the backyard for an hour with a trashy novel, is deeply restorative.

FITNESS If you're not ready to brave the gym or an exercise DVD, start with five girlie pushups (from the knee) in front of the TV set. Each day, challenge yourself to do one more.

FOCUS A pound of muscle burns nine times more calories per day than a pound of fat. You have the power to decrease fat and increase muscle. Choose health.

Homework Assignment
You can't change all your bad habits at once. Make a list of the ones you know are sabotaging you the most. Focus on making gradual changes. For instance, if you're eating all day at your computer, what are some steps you can take to gain control over the situation? First, do your best to add up the calories you're likely consuming every day at your desk. Multiply the daily total by the number of days a week you're transgressing. How many pounds a year are those calories contributing?

Computer-buffet habit buster: today, cut back every snack at the keyboard by 10 percent. Tomorrow, swap a junk snack for something really healthy. The next day, switch out two bad choices for better ones and drink a bottle of water before every no-no snack. Finally, ditch unaccounted-for computer snacking altogether. Divide your lunch in half and eat the remainder of it at your computer over the course of several hours. Chart your progress and collect rewards.

YOUR GAME PLAN (STATE YOUR FOOD AND EXERCISE GOALS FOR THE WEEK)

Gourmet Asparagus, Prosciutto, and Provolone Pizza

SERVES 6 TO 8 *Makes 1 thick-crust 10-inch pizza or 2 thin-crust 8-inch pizzas.*

Decadence doesn't equal diet disaster when you practice portion control. I can't think of a more indulgent supper to have when you're in the mood for really great pizza.

½ **recipe for Mostly Whole-Wheat Pizza Dough (see Week 23) or store-bought whole-wheat pizza dough**

All-purpose flour for sprinkling

Cornmeal for sprinkling

6 **asparagus spears, ends trimmed, very thinly sliced**

¼ **pound imported Italian prosciutto**

⅓ **cup loosely packed grated aged provolone cheese**

FOLLOW directions for shaping and baking dough.

ADD asparagus, prosciutto, and cheese one at a time.

SLIDE dough onto a cookie sheet or pizza stone and place on bottom rack of oven. Bake on highest setting for 5 to 8 minutes, or until golden.

GET ADDICTED— GRADUALLY

Instead of thinking of things in terms of good and bad behavior, focus instead on ways you can improve your surroundings to help facilitate the changes you're aspiring to make. For instance, if you "never" eat breakfast because you "hate" breakfast foods, keep stocking your cupboards with new cereals, switch from gao otation brand milk to milk from a local dairy. Picture that poured over your cereal or splashed into a cup of delicious hot coffee. Splurge on blueberries if that's what it's going to take to lure you into indulging.

What I ate:

What I wish I hadn't:

What I did for exercise:

Tuesday

What I ate:

What I wish I hadn't:

What I did for exercise:

Wednesday

What I ate:

What I wish I hadn't:

What I did for exercise:

Thursday

What I ate:

What I wish I hadn't:

What I did for exercise:

Friday

What I ate:

What I wish I hadn't:

What I did for exercise:

Saturday

I REALLY FELT GREAT WHEN I

What I ate:

What I wish I hadn't:

I CAN GET BETTER AT

What I did for exercise:

NEW FOODS I'M GOING TO TRY

Sunday

What I ate:

What I wish I hadn't:

NEXT WEEK I'M GOING TO

What I did for exercise:

GIVE YOURSELF A GRADE
FOR THIS WEEK'S EFFORTS:

If we weren't meant to eat brightly colored fruits and vegetables every day, they never would have been invented. All those colors mean something. At the risk of getting really technical and boring, suffice it to say that among other important health benefits, fruits and vegetables contain important phytonutrients that aid in cancer prevention and reduce your risk of heart disease. Eat as many brightly colored fruits and veggies as you can, and your body will reciprocate with a pot of gold.

kd@chefkathleen.com

SUBJECT: BARE-BONES WEIGHT-TRAINING FACTS

FROM: Zoe

TO: kd@chefkathleen.com

Dear Kathleen,
What is the difference between weight-bearing exercises and resistance exercises? My doctor is concerned that I may get osteoporosis. Why do these exercises matter?
*   Zoe*

REPLY: REASONS TO RESIST

Dear Zoe,
Both will strengthen your bones. Exercises requiring muscle strength, such as weightlifting and yoga, are considered resistance exercises. Exercises that require your feet to bear the weight of your body, such as walking, climbing stairs, square dancing, and jogging are weight bearing. My mother says weight-bearing and resistance exercises are important "so I can continue doing everything around the house your father refuses to do anymore." Her doctor says they're important to strengthen her bones and help her maintain balance. For more information about osteoporosis, log on to www.nof.org.
    Kathleen

FOOD **No time to cook?** Dice a few kiwis, halve a few grapes, add the juice of a lime, a little chopped cilantro, a teaspoon of grated jalapeño or a dash of hot sauce, season to taste with salt and pepper, and serve with chicken, fish, or thinly sliced beef. That wasn't so hard, was it?

FUN It's best to consume whole fruits and veggies, but there's more than one way to fulfill your daily quota. **Go to a juice bar or gourmet market and try a really funky juice drink.**

FITNESS Drop down and do five pushups and twenty-five crunches. **Stand up and do ten jumping jacks.** Extra credit: do them every day this week.

FOCUS **You can work out till you're blue in the face, but if your diet doesn't follow, you'll never achieve the results you're seeking.**

Homework Assignment Lose an extra pound this week. Weigh-in/ Waistband Wednesdays can either show a gain or a loss; it's up to you. There are 3500 calories in a pound. Cut 250 or burn 250. Burn them through more move- ment: walk, ride, run, swim, dance, wash your windows, detail your car, paint your fence, mow your lawn with a push mower (usually available at garage sales for $2), bunny hop or Hula-Hoop. Cut 250 calories: skip a candy bar, a small vanilla cone, a Venti no-whip skim mocha, half of that healthy-sounding 600- calorie bran muffin, and all the extra bites at mealtimes. Do this every day, seven days in a row, and you'll be a prizewinning loser.

YOUR GAME PLAN (STATE YOUR FOOD AND EXERCISE GOALS FOR THE WEEK)

Pan-Fried Stuffed Chicken with Prosciutto, Mozzarella, and Basil

SERVES 4 *Restaurant-sexy, no culinary degree required: this dress-for-success(ful entertaining) recipe can be made a day in advance up to the point of cooking.*

- ¾ **pound boneless, skinless chicken breast**
- 4 **slices prosciutto**
- 2 **ounces fresh mozzarella cheese, sliced into quarters**
- 8 **basil leaves plus ¼ cup thinly sliced basil leaves**
- 2 **teaspoons olive oil**
- ½ **cup chicken broth**
- I **garlic clove, minced**
- 2 **tablespoons honey mustard**

CUT chicken into 4 pieces, then cut a slit in the side of each piece big enough to stuff. Place a slice of prosciutto, a slice of cheese, and 2 whole basil leaves inside each piece of chicken.

HEAT oil in a large nonstick pan over medium-high until hot but not smoking. Add chicken, reduce heat to medium, and cook for 3 minutes. Turn chicken and cook for 3 to 4 minutes more, or until chicken is completely cooked through. Remove to a serving platter.

ADD chicken broth, garlic, and mustard to pan, bring to a boil, and cook on high until slightly thickened, 1 to 2 minutes. Turn off heat and add sliced basil. Pour over chicken and serve.

Monday

What I ate:

What I wish I hadn't:

What I did for exercise:

Tuesday

What I ate:

What I wish I hadn't:

What I did for exercise:

Wednesday

What I ate:

What I wish I hadn't:

What I did for exercise:

Thursday

What I ate:

What I wish I hadn't:

What I did for exercise:

Friday

What I ate:

What I wish I hadn't:

What I did for exercise:

REPORT CARD

I REALLY FELT GREAT WHEN I

What I ate:

What I wish I hadn't:

I CAN GET BETTER AT

What I did for exercise:

NEW FOODS I'M GOING TO TRY

What I ate:

What I wish I hadn't:

NEXT WEEK I'M GOING TO

What I did for exercise:

GIVE YOURSELF A GRADE
FOR THIS WEEK'S EFFORTS:

I wonder what the guy dipping his chicken nugget into BBQ sauce at 7:50 A.M. was thinking as he swerved to avoid hitting me. I was on my bike, in the bike lane—and he was too. He didn't hit me. Obviously no one had made him breakfast. I wondered what drove him to choose nuggets and sauce as his first source of nourishment for the day ahead. I used to do that: dark chocolate cake and high-octane coffee with full-fat cream was my on-the-go breakfast of choice. I made choices every day that supported ill health. Now I make better choices. Changing your mind, choosing health, is the first step toward gaining control over your life.

kd@chefkathleen.com

SUBJECT: ALL JUNKED UP
FROM: Julie
TO: kd@chefkathleen.com

Dear Kathleen,
I want to lose weight, but I'll be honest with you: all I eat is junk. I don't even know how to start to change my ways.
   Julie

REPLY: NO-JUNK ZONES

Dear Julie,
Make your home a no-junk zone. Don't buy any more of it for the house. No junk cereals, no junk snacks, no junk anything. Creating a situation that forces you to go out and buy junk when you're in the mood for it forces you to make a conscious choice to do so. When you're ready for phase two, make your work environment a no-junk zone. Graduate to "no junk food out" and "no carryout junk food" when you're ready.
   Kathleen

FOOD Pretend there are cameras recording every item you put in your grocery cart this week and that you will be rewarded financially for everything healthy in the cart. **Don't pretend things are healthy when they're not.** Lie-detector sensors will sound louder than a fire engine's siren right there in aisle 4. For a hit-the-jackpot, slap-your-taste-buds-to-attention side dish, grab some baby bok choy (about 1 pound for four), 2 tablespoons low-sodium soy sauce, 1 to 1½ teaspoons Vietnamese chili paste (or a pinch red pepper flakes), and juice of half a lemon. Slice bok choy in half lengthwise, place in a shallow microwave-safe baking dish with 2 tablespoons water, cover loosely with plastic wrap, and microwave on high for 5 minutes. Toss with soy sauce, chili paste, and lemon juice.

FUN **Go to a consignment or thrift shop or Wal-Mart and buy an absolutely spot-on cute outfit that fits you perfectly right now.** Plan on it being *way* too big in two months.

FITNESS Choose to work to your potential throughout your entire workout regime today. **No dilly-dallying, no halfhearted effort.** Give 100 percent.

FOCUS **Talk yourself into health until it comes naturally.** Practice makes perfect.

Homework Assignment

Change your mind, change your habits, change your body. How many trips to the dressing-room torture chambers is it going to take for you to change your mind once and for all? Figure out what it's going to take for you to embrace the opportunities you have to take control of your health.

If you think you'll benefit from a few sessions with a counselor, make an appointment. If you think joining a support group will help you stay on track, join one. If you think keeping a journal will help keep you accountable, start writing.

Reach for your tools and get busy. Run, don't walk.

YOUR GAME PLAN (STATE YOUR FOOD AND EXERCISE GOALS FOR THE WEEK)

Summer Berry Whips

SERVES 4 *This dessert is extremely refreshing in the summertime when berries are plentiful and at their juicy peak, and it's also nice to have around to satisfy your sweet tooth. Stealing a bite of it in the middle of the night won't set you back.*

½ **envelope unflavored gelatin (1 teaspoon)**

2 **cups hulled strawberries, quartered (about 12 ounces)**

1 **cup raspberries (about 5 ounces)**

2 **tablespoons sugar (or more to taste)**

3 **tablespoons fresh lemon juice**
  Dollop of whipped cream or nondairy whipped topping

■ *For fancy company, serve in martini glasses.*

POUR 2 tablespoons cold water into a small bowl. Sprinkle in gelatin and let stand until softened, about 5 minutes. Place strawberries and raspberries, sugar, lemon juice, and ¼ cup water in a 2-quart saucepan over medium-high heat. Bring to a boil, stirring constantly to dissolve sugar. Reduce to a steady simmer and cook for 3 to 4 minutes, or until strawberries have softened a little and raspberries have turned mostly to juice. Add gelatin mixture and cook for 1 minute more, or until gelatin has completely dissolved. Remove from heat and let cool down.

DIVIDE berry mixture among parfait, wine, or champagne glasses and top with whipped cream. Refrigerate until chilled completely, 3 to 4 hours. Serve.

BOK CHOY

Bok choy, a leafy, cabbagelike vegetable, looks more like a head of Swiss chard with white stems than a head of green cabbage. It adds a mild cabbagy flavor and a lot of bulk to the finished dish, making it a great base vegetable. It's terrific in stir-fries because after washing it and shaking it dry, all you have to do is run a knife through it and throw it in the pan. It's an excellent source of vitamin C, folic acid, calcium, beta-carotene, and fiber.

Monday

What I ate:

What I wish I hadn't:

What I did for exercise:

Tuesday

What I ate:

What I wish I hadn't:

What I did for exercise:

Wednesday

What I ate:

What I wish I hadn't:

What I did for exercise:

Thursday

What I ate:

What I wish I hadn't:

What I did for exercise:

Friday

What I ate:

What I wish I hadn't:

What I did for exercise:

Saturday

I REALLY FELT GREAT WHEN I

What I ate:

What I wish I hadn't:

I CAN GET BETTER AT

What I did for exercise:

NEW FOODS I'M GOING TO TRY

Sunday

What I ate:

What I wish I hadn't:

NEXT WEEK I'M GOING TO

What I did for exercise:

GIVE YOURSELF A GRADE
FOR THIS WEEK'S EFFORTS:

Food that's good for you makes you feel good. Nobody binges on broccoli and says, "I need a nap." Junk-food highs lead to health lows. Do you want to hear "See you next year for your annual physical" or do you want to spend the rest of your life seeing specialists and dealing with conditions you caused yourself?

kd@chefkathleen.com

SUBJECT: WHAT, ME COOK?
FROM: Shelly
TO: kd@chefkathleen.com

Dear Kathleen,
I don't know how to cook. What advice do you have?
*   Shelly*

REPLY: FROM WANNABE TO CAN-DO

Dear Shelly,
5 Tips for Wannabe Cooks:

1. Invite yourself over to your mom's house or a friend's to watch her cook.

2. Pick up a cookbook with short ingredient lists and simple instructions. Choose a recipe and try to imagine yourself completing the tasks. Make a grocery list. A day ahead, shop for your provisions.

3. Cook on a day you have time. There's nothing worse than being rushed or feeling pressured when you're trying to learn something new.

4. Make notes directly on the recipe as you cook: about how things taste, what you might do differently next time, how long it took to make, and whether you'd make it again.

5. Start a recipe box or notebook of the recipes you enjoy.

Happy cooking, Shelly.
Kathleen

`FOOD` **You are what you eat.** Do you want to be Duchess Donut, Marshmallow Mandy, Cereal Bar Bonnie, or Olga Oatmeal, Queen of Low Cholesterol?

`FUN` Go to the grocery store. **As a reward for not buying any junk, get in the longest line and read the tabloids.**

`FITNESS` I'll never get rid of my underarm flab. I'm convinced it's there in case I get thrown off a cliff and need to flap my way to safety. **But strong triceps could come in handy, so I do chair dips a couple of times a week.** Sit on the edge of a sturdy chair, place one hand on either side of your hips. Place your legs out in front of you, bend your knees, and slowly bring your hips off the chair and out in front of you. Lower your body by bending your elbows at a 90-degree angle. Keep your body close to the chair. Slowly push up until your arms are straight but not hyperextended. Repeat as many times as you can until you feel like collapsing. I'm kidding! Start with five reps and challenge yourself to do more each time.

`FOCUS` For heaven's sake. **do you want to get rid of the weight or not?** Make every choice count today.

Homework Assignment Do this with your kids if you can. Go through some of the junk food in your house and read through the ingredient lists. Talk about how the empty calories are not serving you nutritionally and how they may be contributing to sugar highs and lows, unnecessary fatigue, ill-fitting jeans, performance issues, moodiness, and less than ideal health. Talk about healthy foods you like and their positive impact. Write down how you think junk calories can hurt you over time and how good foods will impact you long-term. Post everyone's comments on your refrigerator.

YOUR GAME PLAN (STATE YOUR FOOD AND EXERCISE GOALS FOR THE WEEK)

Chicken Mushroom Stir-Fry

SERVES 6 *Stir-fries are the perfect excuse to work in a whole bunch of veggies. Mix and match them to your heart's desire. If you don't like shiitake mushrooms, or your family "won't" eat them, use white or brown button mushrooms.*

- 1 **cup brown rice**
- 1 **cup chicken broth**
- 3 **tablespoons hoisin sauce**
- 2 **tablespoons grated ginger**
- 1 **garlic clove, grated**
- 2 **teaspoons sesame oil**
- ¾ **pound boneless, skinless chicken breast, lightly pounded, cut into thin strips**
- 1 **tablespoon cornstarch, mixed with 1 tablespoon water**
- 3 **ounces shiitake mushrooms, thinly sliced**
- ½ **pound snow peas, trimmed**
- ¾ **pound bean sprouts**

COOK rice in a large pot of boiling water until done, about 25 minutes. Drain and cover.

MIX chicken broth, hoisin, ginger, and garlic in a small bowl. Meanwhile, heat oil in a large nonstick skillet over medium-high heat until hot but not smoking. Add chicken and cook, turning, for 2 minutes. Add broth mixture, stirring often until sauce has thickened slightly, for about 5 minutes. Stir in cornstarch mixture and cook for about 1 minute. Add the mushrooms, snow peas, and bean sprouts, cook, stirring often, for 2 to 3 minutes. Serve over rice.

■ *If you'll "never" prep veggies from scratch, use frozen vegetable medley or splurge on sliced, chopped, and diced salad-bar veggies.*

MUSHROOM MAGIC

A ⅔-cup portion of mushrooms (about 2 ounces) has only 14 measly calories, a tiny ½ gram of fat, no cholesterol, and very little sodium. They're a source of fill-you-up fiber and deliver some hard-to-get essential nutrients: phosphorus (important for bone health), magnesium (necessary for bone, muscle, nerve, and heart health), potassium (important for regulating blood pressure), and selenium (which plays an important role in the immune system).

The best spur-of-the-moment lunch I ever had was served up to me by my good friend Doe in the kitchen of her Boston home: mushrooms sautéed in good olive oil with loads of sliced garlic and fresh thyme all stuffed neatly into a perfectly cooked omelet topped with dollops of whipped goat cheese.

Monday

What I ate:

What I wish I hadn't:

What I did for exercise:

Tuesday

What I ate:

What I wish I hadn't:

What I did for exercise:

Wednesday

What I ate:

What I wish I hadn't:

What I did for exercise:

Thursday

What I ate:

What I wish I hadn't:

What I did for exercise:

Friday

What I ate:

What I wish I hadn't:

What I did for exercise:

REPORT CARD

I REALLY FELT GREAT WHEN I

I CAN GET BETTER AT

NEW FOODS I'M GOING TO TRY

NEXT WEEK I'M GOING TO

GIVE YOURSELF A GRADE
FOR THIS WEEK'S EFFORTS:

Saturday

What I ate:

What I wish I hadn't:

What I did for exercise:

Sunday

What I ate:

What I wish I hadn't:

What I did for exercise:

Dog Days of Summer Chow

A month of 80-degrees-before-breakfast days is not a legitimate reason to take a hiatus from health, abandon real food for ice cream, and skip exercise. Plan for days when you're too tired, hot, or lazy to cook.

kd@chefkathleen.com

SUBJECT: IF YOU CAN'T STAND THE HEAT…

FROM: Elke
TO: kd@chefkathleen.com

Dear Kathleen,
I look for any excuse not to cook.
I hate turning my oven on in the summer. Any suggestions?
Elke

REPLY: TAKE REFUGE IN THE DEEP FREEZE

Dear Elke,
I have a freezer full of reheat-and-eat Chef Kathleen–made TV dinners — meals I've portioned out and frozen for days I don't feel like cooking. I invite people over for BBQs if they'll run the grill. Mostly, I make a lot of salads, vegetable frittatas, and omelets in the summer and include revitalizing fruits in as many meals as possible.

5 Cool Ways to Work Fruit into Warm-Weather Menus:

1. Think fruit salsas and serve them with grilled meat, chicken, and fish.

2. Serve fruit salad on a stick – fruit kebabs are a great make-ahead crowd-pleaser, perfect for outdoor entertaining.

3. Serve a plain chicken salad in half a papaya or throw some pineapple on the grill to have with chicken or fish.

4. Add grapes and strawberries to chicken or shrimp salad and serve on a bed of lettuces with more grapes and strawberries.

5. Visit U-pick farms all season long. You'll be forced to think out of the recipe box! Log on to chefkathleen.com for recipes.

Kathleen

FOOD Fruit-on-a-stick can be made with absolutely any fruit you like and can be tailored to children or dressed up for adults. **Kebabs can be made to stand alone or designed to dip in fruit-flavored yogurt or melted dark chocolate.** Use bamboo skewers, or rosemary branches, or sugarcane. My favorite fruit-on-a-stick combos: strawberries, pineapple, and grapes; melon and blueberries squeezed with fresh lemon juice; raspberries, blackberries, strawberries, and angel food cake squares for dipping in dark chocolate; and strawberries, blueberries, and star-fruit slices for Memorial Day, Fourth of July, and Labor Day.

FUN **Get a new BBQ cookbook to inspire you to cook outside.** My brother fires up his Weber even in the dead of Michigan winters. He stands out there in shorts and snow boots and merrily cooks for his family.

FITNESS **Hot days, keep-cool exercise options:** exercise early in the morning, exercise after sundown, go to the gym when it's not crowded, go swimming, play in the sprinklers with the kids, go jump in a lake and tread water, go to a water park. Wear sunscreen. Stay hydrated.

FOCUS **The consequences of too many days off from exercise, along with poor choices, stack up quickly.**

Homework Assignment Make a list of weather-related excuses. Can't think of any? How about it's too hot, it's too cold, it's too drizzly, it's too windy, it looks like it *might* rain, it's snowing. Hang it on the bathroom mirror next to the cutest picture you have of yourself and don't let that baby down!

YOUR GAME PLAN (STATE YOUR FOOD AND EXERCISE GOALS FOR THE WEEK)

Nectarine and Peach Batter Cobbler

SERVES 6 TO 8 *I've cut back on the butter, flour, and sugar in this heavenly cobbler, making it the perfect recipe for people who will accept no substitutes when it comes to dessert.*

FOR THE FRUIT

2½ **pounds nectarines and peaches, preferably white (about 6 large), peeled, pitted, and cut into ¼-inch-thick slices**

1 **tablespoon fresh lemon juice**

½ **cup sugar**

FOR THE BATTER

3 **tablespoons unsalted butter**

½ **cup all-purpose flour**

¼ **cup plus 2 tablespoons sugar**

2 **teaspoons baking powder**

⅛ **teaspoon salt**

½ **cup 2% milk**

PREHEAT oven to 375°F.

FRUIT: Place fruit, lemon juice, and sugar in a medium nonaluminum saucepan. Bring to a boil, stirring constantly, until fruit creates enough juice so that you don't have to stir constantly. Cook, stirring occasionally, for 6 minutes, or until fruit has completely softened and has started to thicken. Remove from heat.

BATTER: Melt butter and pour into a 9-inch baking pan. Whisk together flour, sugar, baking powder, and salt. Using a fork, stir in milk until just combined. Pour into baking pan; do not stir. Pour fruit into pan; do not stir.

PLACE in oven and cook until fruit is jam-thick and the top is golden brown, 35 to 40 minutes. Set pan on a rack until warm, 15 to 20 minutes.

■ *You need to peel the peaches and nectarines, which you can easily do ahead of time. Bring to a boil a pot of water large enough to hold the fruit. Turn off heat. Carefully place pot with water in sink. Add fruit. Let stand 15 to 30 seconds. Pour off water. Using the tip of a small paring knife or your fingers, gently peel off skin and discard.*

DARE TO EAT A PEACH (OR NECTARINE)

White peaches and nectarines are sweeter than yellow because they have lower acid levels. But it's more important to choose the fruit that looks and smells the best. Skins should be smooth and blemish-free. The fruit should give the tiniest bit when you gently press your finger into the flesh at the top or stem end and should be pleasantly fragrant.

5 Favorite Ways to Enjoy Peaches and Nectarines

5. Slice and toss with blueberries in a bowl with cherry vanilla yogurt and your favorite granola.

4. Bake in a crisp or cobbler when company's coming.

3. Peel, slice, lightly smash, and serve on a little bit of real vanilla ice cream.

2. Slice and toss with lime, cilantro, salt, and pepper and serve over grilled white fish.

1. Eat a drip-down-your-arm really great one in the shade of a tree.

Monday

What I ate:

What I wish I hadn't:

What I did for exercise:

Tuesday

What I ate:

What I wish I hadn't:

What I did for exercise:

Wednesday

What I ate:

What I wish I hadn't:

What I did for exercise:

Thursday

What I ate:

What I wish I hadn't:

What I did for exercise:

Friday

What I ate:

What I wish I hadn't:

What I did for exercise:

Saturday

I REALLY FELT GREAT WHEN I

What I ate:

What I wish I hadn't:

I CAN GET BETTER AT

What I did for exercise:

NEW FOODS I'M GOING TO TRY

Sunday

What I ate:

What I wish I hadn't:

NEXT WEEK I'M GOING TO

What I did for exercise:

GIVE YOURSELF A GRADE
FOR THIS WEEK'S EFFORTS:

WEEK 30
Prepare to Win and You Will

You can act like a sloth or you can embrace the opportunities before you. I went cycling recently with an elite group of riders. I fell in the first minute. I was the worst, most-out-of-shape rider on the planet. Because the group's fitness level exceeded my own, I pushed myself mentally and physically. At the end of the ride, the team invited me to join them again. My mind wanted to decline politely, but my inner goddess of fitness began to think of ways I could prepare. Focusing on eating healthy, staying hydrated, getting proper rest, and maintaining my bike helped me gain the confidence I needed to say yes. Find ways to push yourself out of your comfort zone and take yourself to the next level. Ready, get set, *go!*

kd@chefkathleen.com

SUBJECT: WORK LIKE A DOG…

FROM: Taylor

TO: kd@chefkathleen.com

Dear Kathleen,
I am always starving after my workouts. What do you eat when you're training?
Taylor

REPLY: BUT DON'T EAT LIKE ONE!

Dear Taylor,
The cookies and candy I crave and feel that I *deserve* after a ride do nothing to help my body recover or prepare for the next ride. Whether I'm training or not, I make efforts to work in as many fruits, whole grains, legumes, and other vegetables as I can. You should also include lean protein, low-fat dairy, and, yes, the occasional splurge. What fun would life be without ice cream cones?
Kathleen

FOOD Increase good carbs this week. **Make a list of the carbs you're consuming and fill in the blanks.** How many legumes have *you* added to menus lately? How about sneaking an extra serving of veggies into dinner every night this week?

FUN **Invite over your best friends for a bring-your-own-healthy-supper potluck and play bunco way past your bedtime.**

FITNESS Make a mental list of where you're at fitnesswise. **What's the next logical level for you?** If you're doing thirty minutes on the treadmill with no incline at a speed of 3.5 and you're feeling good there, step it up! Go to an incline of 1 and increase your speed to 4. See how long you can keep it up.

FOCUS Practice turning negative internal dialogue into positive. **You do not have to accept self-sabotage as a tenant in your head.** You're the landlord.

Homework Assignment Figure out a way to work out with an individual or group of people who are at a slightly higher skill level than you. If you work out at home, pursue working out with a partner once a week. Invite someone to come over and work out with you, or schedule a weekly power walk with a fit friend. Consider signing up for a class. If a month of classes is intimidating, sign up for a one-time-only gig.

YOUR GAME PLAN (STATE YOUR FOOD AND EXERCISE GOALS FOR THE WEEK)

Binge Pickles

MAKES 8 CUPS *How much of a pickle can you get into by eating some? Even if they do have a little sugar in the brine, we're not talking a bag of chips or cookies. Use any kind of veggies you like.*

2 **cups cider vinegar**

½ **cup sugar**

1 **teaspoon salt**

1 **tablespoon cumin seeds**

½ **teaspoon red pepper flakes, or more or less to taste**

1 **bay leaf**

5 **whole cloves**

1 **teaspoon whole peppercorns**

1 **teaspoon fennel seeds**

1 **2-inch piece ginger, peeled and very thinly sliced**

Lemon zest peeled from ½ lemon

2 **large carrots, peeled and cut into ¼-inch-thick sticks**

½ **pound green beans, trimmed and cut into bite-size pieces**

2 **medium cucumbers, quartered, seeded, and trimmed to length of carrot sticks**

½ **pound asparagus, tough ends snapped off, stems peeled**

PLACE vinegar, 2 cups water, sugar, salt, spices, ginger, and lemon zest in a large nonreactive saucepan over high heat. Bring to a boil, whisking, until sugar is dissolved. Remove from heat and cool brine completely.

PLACE carrots and green beans in a shallow dish with 2 tablespoons water. Cover loosely with plastic and microwave on high until al dente, about 2 minutes. Cool slightly. Place vegetables in a Mason jar or refrigerator dish. Add cucumber sticks, asparagus, and brine. Refrigerate covered overnight. The pickled vegetables keep for about 3 weeks.

■ *You can use a vegetable peeler to peel the lemon so you get nice big pieces of peel, and you can also use it to peel the ginger.* ■ *To seed the cucumbers, scoop them out with a spoon.*

WEIGHT-LOSS NIGHTCAP

Weight-loss success story, Carol Daelemans, who has lost 40 pounds and counting, attributes part of her results to working out with her best friend. "We get together nearly every evening to walk two to six miles. We walk in heat, darkness, and even rain. It's not just exercise, it's therapy. Every day we get out of the house, get away from our families, and vent. Where would any woman be without the support of her girl-friends?"

Monday

What I ate:

What I wish I hadn't:

What I did for exercise:

Tuesday

What I ate:

What I wish I hadn't:

What I did for exercise:

Wednesday

What I ate:

What I wish I hadn't:

What I did for exercise:

Thursday

What I ate:

What I wish I hadn't:

What I did for exercise:

Friday

What I ate:

What I wish I hadn't:

What I did for exercise:

REPORT CARD

I REALLY FELT GREAT WHEN I

I CAN GET BETTER AT

NEW FOODS I'M GOING TO TRY

NEXT WEEK I'M GOING TO

GIVE YOURSELF A GRADE
FOR THIS WEEK'S EFFORTS:

Saturday

What I ate:

What I wish I hadn't:

What I did for exercise:

Sunday

What I ate:

What I wish I hadn't:

What I did for exercise:

It's OK to bend the rules sometimes, as long as you're mostly playing the game, but when you get to that tired stage and you bend the rules so much that they break, you've started a new game. It's called the weight-gain game. That little piece of chocolate measures zero on the ounce scale, so three pieces must register zero too. The definition of a cup keeps getting bigger. Tasting while you're cooking doesn't count either. When you first start dieting, you make every portion a little bit smaller. When you're bending the rules, everything starts getting bigger and bigger, until you do too.

kd@chefkathleen.com

SUBJECT: THE WALKING BORED

FROM: Keiley

TO: kd@chefkathleen.com

Dear Kathleen,
I need to walk, but I get bored really easily. Any thoughts on how to keep myself motivated?
    Keiley

REPLY: WALK AMERICA!

Dear Keiley,
Success story Elfinlady has the perfect prescription for you: "To keep things interesting, I find out how far it is from my house to my destination. I plot my route on a map hanging in my kitchen. I have a pedometer that I wear all day long as I walk around at work. At the end of each day, I tally up my pedometer miles along with cardio miles accrued at the gym. I log the miles on my map with colored highlighters. For every 10 miles I walk, I add $5 to a jar. When I get to each destination, I treat myself to something with the money I've earned: a haircut, a piece of clothing, or a trip to the movies."

    Kathleen

FOOD Extra food is your enemy when you're in Rule-Bender Rebound Boot Camp. **Every bite counts, so count every bite.** For a delicious dessert, sprinkle peach or nectarine halves with a tiny bit of sugar and put them under a hot broiler.

FUN **Go online and shop luxuriously.** Go to all those stores you feel out of place in. I hit Tiffany, Neiman Marcus, and Barneys New York and fill my "cart" with thousands of dollars worth of items I can't possibly afford and don't need anyway. Pretending is fat-free fun.

FITNESS Reassess your workout habits too. Sick to death of your yoga tape? **Get a Pilates tape.** Sick of the StairMaster? Run to the treadmill.

FOCUS Don't quit. Don't entertain negative internal dialogue. **Stay the course and keep the pace.** Your pace. You *will* make it.

Homework Assignment

Homework Assignment Start Week 1 again. Get out the measuring spoons, measuring cups, and the kitchen scale. Spend a week being 100 percent honest with the quantity of food you're consuming. Write down everything you eat, including samples, kids-plate scraps, and "tastes" while you're cooking.

YOUR GAME PLAN (STATE YOUR FOOD AND EXERCISE GOALS FOR THE WEEK)

Guilt-Free Vanilla Gelato

SERVES 6 *OK, so it's not exactly ice cream, but make this recipe on a hot day and serve it the minute it's churned enough to eat, and you'll give up the store-bought version of the "real" thing. This gelato is made from whole milk instead of cream and doesn't have eggs. Of course you have to mind your portion sizes, but what's new?*

If you've always wondered what gives the best vanilla ice creams that authentic vanilla flavor, it's vanilla bean.

4 **cups whole milk**

I **cup sugar**

I **vanilla bean pod, split in half lengthwise, or I teaspoon pure vanilla extract**

7 **teaspoons cornstarch**

POUR 1 cup milk into a medium bowl and add sugar. Scrape vanilla bean seeds with the tip of a small knife into mixture or add extract. Add cornstarch and stir until combined.

POUR remaining 3 cups milk and vanilla bean pod into a medium heavy-bottomed saucepan and bring to a simmer over medium heat. Remove from heat and stir in sugar mixture. Cook over medium-low heat, stirring constantly, until mixture comes to a boil and thickens slightly, about 10 minutes. Refrigerate for 2 to 3 hours or overnight. Process in an ice cream maker according to manufacturer's directions. Serve.

■ *You can find vanilla bean pods in gourmet grocery stores, but they're pricey. If you're not in the mood to shop and spend, use pure vanilla extract instead.*

Monday

What I ate:

What I wish I hadn't:

What I did for exercise:

Tuesday

What I ate:

What I wish I hadn't:

What I did for exercise:

Wednesday

What I ate:

What I wish I hadn't:

What I did for exercise:

Thursday

What I ate:

What I wish I hadn't:

What I did for exercise:

Friday

What I ate:

What I wish I hadn't:

What I did for exercise:

REPORT CARD

I REALLY FELT GREAT WHEN I

I CAN GET BETTER AT

NEW FOODS I'M GOING TO TRY

NEXT WEEK I'M GOING TO

GIVE YOURSELF A GRADE
FOR THIS WEEK'S EFFORTS:

Saturday

What I ate:

What I wish I hadn't:

What I did for exercise:

Sunday

What I ate:

What I wish I hadn't:

What I did for exercise:

It's hard to stay on track with food and fitness when there are a million reasons for why doing so is "just too much right now." Putting things into perspective helps. Humbling yourself helps even more. It's irresponsible to waste the gifts and freedoms you're granted each day. It's not always easy to stay in tune with this belief, but it's one of the first realizations I try to bring to the surface when I'm pity-partying hard.

kd@chefkathleen.com

SUBJECT: I CAN'T CATCH UP!
FROM: Tracey
TO: kd@chefkathleen.com

Dear Kathleen,
I'm taking care of my parents, who are both in their eighties and live with us. I have two small children and a husband who can't pick up after himself. My house is a mess. I'm always in my car driving someone somewhere. I need to lose sixty pounds. Help!
Tracey

REPLY: PLAY BALL!

Dear Tracey,
You certainly have the weight of the world on your shoulders, but I encourage you to enlist a team of experts to absorb some of the responsibilities you're faced with. Log on to aarp.org to find your local chapter, which can help you learn what services are available in your community. Support could include home health aides, shopping assistants, a housekeeper, a handyman, meal services, and referral programs.

In the meantime, take care of *your* health needs first. Food can give the energy edge you need, so eat right. Schedule play dates for yourself—time away from all your responsibilities to have fun. Exercise releases the feel-good hormones you need right now, so don't skip your workouts! Eliminating some of the stresses will allow you to get the rest, exercise, and nutrition you need to get back on track. Take things a day at a time, Tracey.
Kathleen

FOOD Take a tropical getaway on the cheap. Chunks of icy cold, ripe pineapple with lime sorbet is a wonderful any-time-of-year treat. Serve it up resort-style using your best china and climb into the comfiest chair you have. **Turn off the phones, close your doors, and mute mental chatter.** Relax and enjoy.

FUN Send everyone outside, including the dog, set the timer for 15 minutes, sit down, and read chapter one of a new book. **Give yourself a chapter time-out every day.** It might take you a month to get through a book, but that's not the point.

FITNESS Having a stash of exercise DVDs really helps. I have eight-, twenty-, thirty-, and sixty-minute workouts to choose from. If I get five minutes in, I talk myself into five more by setting rewards along the way. The longer I go, the greater the rewards.

FOCUS Exercise doesn't need to be Ironman madness. **Give yourself permission to take the day off from hard exercise.** Allowing yourself to indulge in twenty minutes of something peaceful and relaxing can be deeply restorative.

Homework Assignment

Nothing will make you feel more in control than taking control. Make a list of ten things in your life that you're really thankful for. Now make a list of ten things you've always wanted to do. Read your lists every morning. The things on your lists need to happen for real. A promising future makes for a good today. Knowing there are things to look forward to will make you feel better.

YOUR GAME PLAN (STATE YOUR FOOD AND EXERCISE GOALS FOR THE WEEK)

Pesto Primavera Microwave Frittata

SERVES 1 *When you're feeling cereal-for-supper lazy, make this recipe instead. It doesn't take more than 5 minutes.*

4 **large egg whites**
2 **teaspoons store-bought pesto**
  Coarse salt and cracked black pepper to taste
1 **cup salad bar veggies**
1 **tablespoon grated Parmesan cheese**

IN a wide, shallow, microwave-safe soup or pasta bowl, whisk together egg whites, pesto, salt, and pepper. Add veggies and stir until combined.

MICROWAVE on high for 30 seconds. Remove and stir eggs once or twice. Sprinkle with cheese. Return to the microwave and cook on high for 1 minute and 30 seconds, or until done. Serve.

BANANA POWER

Bananas are fill-you-up nutritional powerhouses, containing 20 percent of the U.S. Recommended Daily Allowance of B_6 and 11 percent of potassium. According to the U.S. Food and Drug Administration, eating foods rich in potassium and low in sodium may help to reduce the risk of high blood pressure and stroke.

One of my favorite Help! I'm-starving emergency snacks is a breadless banana–peanut butter sandwich. Slice a banana in half lengthwise, spread with whipped peanut butter, and sprinkle with plump California raisins. For a decadent dessert, swap the raisins for a sprinkling of toasted coconut and dust with a layer of cocoa powder.

What I ate:

What I wish I hadn't:

What I did for exercise:

Tuesday

What I ate:

What I wish I hadn't:

What I did for exercise:

Wednesday

What I ate:

What I wish I hadn't:

What I did for exercise:

Thursday

What I ate:

What I wish I hadn't:

What I did for exercise:

Friday

What I ate:

What I wish I hadn't:

What I did for exercise:

Saturday

What I ate:

What I wish I hadn't:

What I did for exercise:

I REALLY FELT GREAT WHEN I

I CAN GET BETTER AT

NEW FOODS I'M GOING TO TRY

Sunday

What I ate:

What I wish I hadn't:

What I did for exercise:

NEXT WEEK I'M GOING TO

GIVE YOURSELF A GRADE
FOR THIS WEEK'S EFFORTS:

What's Your Weight-Loss Personality?

Couch potatoes, exercise phobics, can't-stand-to-cook-club members, and dropout divas, unite. Unite your determination, your health needs, your abilities, your resources, and your right to happiness. This is about you and what you can do for you. Don't put your health, your happiness, or your fate in someone else's hands. Anybody can have a seat on this bandwagon, so whether you possess the skills or not, pretend that you do, behave like you do, and eventually you will.

5 THINGS YOU CAN DO TO SUCCEED AT WEIGHT LOSS

1. Develop a positive attitude. Whether you believe it or not, tell yourself over and over that you can do this until you've knocked the twenty-four-hour negative internal dialogue channel in your head right off the air. You might have to get up and do this every day for the rest of your life. So what?

2. Participate in a weight-loss program. Sign up for a formal program or design your own, as I did. Create a detailed plan, down to the number of calories you'll consume in a day if that's what it takes, along with the number of minutes you plan to exercise, or commit to improve a habit a day until you've achieved your goals.

3. Set goals. If you don't know what you're working for, how can you succeed? Write down exactly what you want and baby-step your way there.

4. Develop positive coping skills. Master mastering stress and anything else that derails you. Be purposeful. Be results-orientated. Seek the help you need to react positively to everyday challenges. Anticipate the need to modify existing coping skills and to procure new ones as you go.

5. Be physically active. Stretch. Sweat. Stretch. Collect a prize. Repeat.

FOOD **Make tuna kebabs tonight.** Skewer 1-inch cubes of fresh tuna alternately with cubes of pineapple, season with salt and pepper, brush lightly with oil, and grill or pan-sear. Whisk together fresh lime juice, a drizzle of olive oil, some chopped fresh basil and mint, and pour over finished kebabs just before serving.

FUN Plant seeds. Plant a windowsill full of potted herbs or a row of young greens in your garden. **Amend the soil.** Make room for new growth and new life. Nurture the seeds. Weed out unwanted stragglers. Tend to your seeds daily. Watch them blossom. Harvest time is coming.

FITNESS How many abs did you do today? How many more do you have in you? **What are you waiting for?** Drop down and crunch!

FOCUS **Inner resolve: it's in there.** Exercise it.

Homework Assignment Read through the tips for weight-loss success at the beginning of this week's pages and assess where you're at. Determine growth opportunities. Brainstorm baby steps you can take toward healthy ideal behavior in each category. For instance, if you don't have a positive attitude, discuss with your children ways they can work on their own self-esteem issues or counsel a friend. In healing others, we heal ourselves. If you don't have a weight-loss program, why not? Draft one and post it on the forums at chefkathleen.com today!

YOUR GAME PLAN (STATE YOUR FOOD AND EXERCISE GOALS FOR THE WEEK)

Buttermilk Zucchini Corn Muffins with Cheddar and Herbs

MAKES 16 MUFFINS *Sometimes nothing else will do but a warm, savory muffin right from the oven. If you're like me and find it hard to "eat just one," bake when you're expecting a crowd.*

- 1 **cup all-purpose flour**
- ½ **cup whole-wheat pastry flour**
- ¼ **cup cornmeal**
- ½ **teaspoon baking soda**
- 1½ **teaspoons baking powder**
- 1½ **cups low-fat buttermilk**
- 2 **large eggs or 4 egg whites**
- 2 **tablespoons canola oil**
- 1 **teaspoon salt**
- 1 **tablespoon sugar (optional)**
- 1 **cup grated or julienned zucchini**
- 1 **cup fresh corn kernels (about 2 ears)**
- ½ **cup finely grated, very loosely packed extra-sharp cheddar cheese**
- 1 **tablespoon chopped fresh herbs, such as thyme or basil**

PREHEAT oven to 425° F. Grease 16 muffin cups, filling any empty cups with a bit of water. In medium bowl, sift together flours, cornmeal, baking soda, and baking powder and set aside.

IN a large bowl, combine buttermilk, eggs, oil, salt, and sugar, if using. Add zucchini, corn, cheese, and herbs. Stir until just combined.

ADD dry ingredients to wet and stir until just incorporated. Spoon batter into greased muffin tins. Bake for 15 minutes, or until a toothpick inserted into middle comes out clean. Let muffins cool in cups for 10 minutes. Then unmold and serve.

■ *Whole-wheat pastry flour has less gluten than regular whole-wheat flour and makes for more tender baked goods. You can find it in many supermarkets and in health food stores.*

Monday

What I ate:

What I wish I hadn't:

What I did for exercise:

Tuesday

What I ate:

What I wish I hadn't:

What I did for exercise:

Wednesday

What I ate:

What I wish I hadn't:

What I did for exercise:

Thursday

What I ate:

What I wish I hadn't:

What I did for exercise:

Friday

What I ate:

What I wish I hadn't:

What I did for exercise:

Saturday

I REALLY FELT GREAT WHEN I

What I ate:

What I wish I hadn't:

I CAN GET BETTER AT

What I did for exercise:

Sunday

NEW FOODS I'M GOING TO TRY

What I ate:

What I wish I hadn't:

NEXT WEEK I'M GOING TO

What I did for exercise:

GIVE YOURSELF A GRADE
FOR THIS WEEK'S EFFORTS:

Love the body you have every day, all along the way. Either live life as someone who does the best you can or someone who doesn't. There's no dual citizenship. By not changing your image and acknowledging that you're now a stronger, slimmer, fitter, healthier version of yourself, it's too easy to slide back. The key to getting a new self-image is getting rid of the old self-image. Burn your fat-land passport. Donate all your old clothes. Think of this process as you would any other significant passage in your life. Let everyone know, have a party, and plan it like a wedding.

kd@chefkathleen.com

SUBJECT: HEAVY TWIN, HEALTHY TWIN

FROM: Renée

TO: kd@chefkathleen.com

Dear Kathleen,
I've lost 62 pounds. I feel like fraternal twins—fat me, thin me. I've been enjoying the compliments and kudos from friends and family, and I'm proud of what I've done so far, but I still see myself as the same old me and not the one who can go shopping in the same department as my skinny friends. How can I fully appreciate that I'm half the woman I used to be, figuratively speaking?
Renée

REPLY: HAPPY TWIN!

Dear Renée,
Sometimes I still feel like a fraud in regular-people clothes, as if an uptight saleslady is going to force me to return the size 8s. There's a self-esteem bookshop near my house. When I heard about it, I thought I was in a *Seinfeld* episode, but I went and stocked up. Some of the books helped me. Some helped my bookshelf look full. Staying in touch with the reasons you *need* to eat right and exercise and how to do it is important. Learning how to feel good about who you are, who you're becoming, and who you want to leave behind is important too. Access tools.

Kathleen

FOOD **For a decadent new-you supper celebration, pull out all the stops and try something over the top.** One of my favorite decadent salads: finely sliced pears tossed with arugula and Gorgonzola cheese and drizzled with balsamic vinegar and olive oil. For a more substantial meal, serve it with a lightly pounded, very thinly sliced seared breast of boneless, skinless chicken.

FUN Go shopping in regular-people stores. You need to get used to these shops, the sizes they offer, and how the clothes fit your new body. **Don't get hung up on sizes.** They're all over the map. If you like what you see in the mirror, do a happy dance and tell the salesperson to wrap it up.

FITNESS **Protein is essential for muscle recovery.** Getting it from sources that will fuel your body and workouts effectively is essential.

5 Excellent Sources of Protein:

6 ounces canned tuna = 40 grams protein

4 ounces chicken breast = 35 grams protein

3 ounces beef (the size of a deck of cards) = 26 grams protein

3 ounces salmon = 23 grams protein

1 cup cooked black beans = 16 grams protein

FOCUS **Get mad, get even, get thinner, get fitter.**

Homework Assignment Go through your closet and fill up at least one garbage bag with clothes that no longer fit or don't look good on you anymore. Get rid of things you haven't worn, things that aren't your color, and things your family would be embarrassed to see you in. Listen to the new skinny you and keep only those things you like.

YOUR GAME PLAN (STATE YOUR FOOD AND EXERCISE GOALS FOR THE WEEK)

Sausage, Chickpea, and Sweet Potato Stew

SERVES 6 TO 8 *This nutritional powerhouse is a favorite of Katie Couric. She made it for her classmates at a reunion party.*

2 teaspoons olive oil

1 small onion, diced

2 garlic cloves, minced

½ pound Italian sausage, casings removed

1 28-ounce can crushed tomatoes

3 cups chicken broth

1 sweet potato (about 1 pound), peeled and diced into ½-inch chunks

1 teaspoon ground cumin

1 teaspoon fennel seeds, crushed with bottom of a heavy skillet

1 small squash, such as buttercup (about 1½ pounds), peeled, seeded, and diced

1 15-ounce can chickpeas, drained and rinsed

Coarse salt and cracked black pepper

HEAT oil in a large pot over medium-high heat. When hot but not smoking, add onion and garlic. Cook, uncovered, stirring every now and then, until onion has completely softened, 1 to 2 minutes. Add sausage and cook, breaking it apart with a spatula or spoon, until cooked through, 2 to 3 minutes.

ADD tomatoes, broth, sweet potato, cumin, and fennel seeds. Bring to a boil, reduce to a simmer, and cook until sweet potato is almost done, about 10 minutes. Add squash and chickpeas and cook, uncovered, for 15 to 25 minutes more, until squash is fork-tender. Taste, adjust seasonings with salt and pepper, and serve.

■ *To dice squash without losing a limb, poke holes in the squash all over with a knife. Microwave on high for 5 minutes until softened. Cool and remove skin with a sharp carrot peeler or knife. Cut squash in half; scoop out seeds. Cut into ½-inch-thick slices. Stack slices on top of one another in piles. Cut slices crosswise into ½-inch-thick strips. Cut strips into ½-inch chunks. Repeat with remaining squash.*

PICK OF THE CROP

Winter squashes, such as buttercup, acorn, butternut, kabocha, hubbard, and pumpkin are excellent sources of vitamin A (beta-carotene), vitamins B_1, B_3, B_5, and B_6, vitamin C, folate, potassium, and fiber. Getting extra beta-carotene in your diet may help to prevent atherosclerosis.

B vitamins help break down carbohydrates into glucose, which provides energy for the body. They also help break down fats and proteins.

Folate helps our bodies produce and maintain new cells. Potassium can help maintain normal blood pressure and protect against heart disease and stroke.

Dietary fiber helps prevent heart disease, diabetes, and some cancers. It also helps you to feel full. Getting full on the right stuff is how I keep myself from overeating the wrong stuff.

What I ate:

What I wish I hadn't:

What I did for exercise:

Tuesday

What I ate:

What I wish I hadn't:

What I did for exercise:

Wednesday

What I ate:

What I wish I hadn't:

What I did for exercise:

Thursday

What I ate:

What I wish I hadn't:

What I did for exercise:

Friday

What I ate:

What I wish I hadn't:

What I did for exercise:

Saturday

I REALLY FELT GREAT WHEN I

What I ate:

I CAN GET BETTER AT

What I wish I hadn't:

What I did for exercise:

NEW FOODS I'M GOING TO TRY

Sunday

What I ate:

NEXT WEEK I'M GOING TO

What I wish I hadn't:

What I did for exercise:

GIVE YOURSELF A GRADE
FOR THIS WEEK'S EFFORTS:

If your actions are in alignment with your goals, you're on your way. When they're not, you're not. Feeling guilty about what you're not doing is a pointless waste of time, energy, and emotion. Spin your wheels on the treadmill, spin your wheels in the kitchen, spin your wheels to create forward movement. What can you tackle this week that will take you to the next level of health or fitness? Keep your focus small. Be specific. Create accountability, and off you go.

kd@chefkathleen.com

SUBJECT: NO FRILLS
FROM: Emileigh
TO: kd@chefkathleen.com

Dear Kathleen,
What kind of short-term rewards do you use to keep you going? I dream of being a perfect size 6, but that's a year or so away. I need incentives.
Emileigh

REPLY: CHEAP THRILLS

Dear Emileigh,
I have a short attention span when it comes to staying on track and have found that rewards really help me. Because I can't justify or afford to shower myself with a constant stream of gifts, I use everyday things as rewards, except those times when only a little trinket will do.
Cheapskate Rewards — Daily Treats That Must Be Earned:
   * A morning walk through the garden
   * Browsing through the online edition of the *New York Times*
   * A social phone call
   * Flipping through the good mail
   * Reading a non-work-related article start to finish
   * Replying to or initiating social e-mail
My cheapskate rewards system is the only way I've been able to stay on track all these years. Acknowledging positive behavior creates positive feelings.
   Kathleen

FOOD You are in control of your eating. **Repeat after me: "I am in control of my eating."** Practice saying this over and over, especially when you're in the middle of an eating attack. I promise you, it will take the wind out of your wanna-eat-like-a-whale sails.

FUN No matter what day of the week it is, dig around until you can find the weekend section of the newspaper—the one that features art openings, exhibits, concerts, festivals, and f-u-n events taking place in your area. **Circle three activities that appeal to you.** Schedule one. Mark it in your calendar. Extra credit: schedule all three.

FITNESS Females only beyond this point. There's nothing worse than runaway bazoombas. **Pretend that the Queer Eye guys are on their way over to evaluate your gym-lingerie drawer.** Invest in comfortable sports bras made from breathable fabrics that fit you perfectly. Enough with clearance-rack buys that are a size too small or too large. Save money somewhere else.

FOCUS If you intend to succeed at weight loss, act like it and you will.

Homework Assignment The quickest way to get out from underneath the strain and stress of a lousy behavior is to tackle it head-on. Face one of your fears this week. Strategize your way to better behavior. If you've been skipping your workouts, figure out what it is you're willing to do today. Write it down, figure out when you will have the time to do it, and set a reward. Follow through. Make a list of what you're willing to do every day for the rest of this week. Do not sabotage yourself with a holier-than-though workout schedule. Finish your week strong by keeping your goals realistic and achievable.

YOUR GAME PLAN (STATE YOUR FOOD AND EXERCISE GOALS FOR THE WEEK)

Sunday Supper for One

SERVES 1 *This easy-to-get-on-the-table meal showcases the flavors of summer and is perfect for nights when your appetite is greater than your will to cook.*

1 teaspoon olive oil

1 garlic clove, very thinly sliced

10 cherry tomatoes

8–10 spears asparagus, ends trimmed and very thinly sliced

1 small pattypan squash, very thinly sliced or diced

2 sprigs fresh thyme

6–8 leaves fresh oregano or a pinch of dried

Coarse salt and cracked black pepper

2 large eggs

POUR olive oil into a 10-inch nonstick skillet. Add garlic and tomatoes. Turn heat to medium and cook until garlic is fragrant and just starting to turn golden, 2 to 3 minutes.

INCREASE heat to medium-high and add asparagus, squash, and herbs and cook, tossing often, until vegetables are just done, 3 to 4 minutes. Season to taste with salt and pepper. Pour onto a serving plate.

PLACE pan back on burner and add eggs. Fry until just done, 2 to 3 minutes. Season to taste with salt and pepper. Slide eggs onto veggies. Serve immediately.

OREGANO

Oregano is a member of the mint family. Two "flavors" are widely available: Mexican and Turkish (sometimes also called Greek or Mediterranean). Mexican oregano is sharper, more pungent, and less sweet, making it well suited for spicy dishes like chili. Turkish oregano, used in Italian and Italian-American cooking, is pleasantly sweet and mild, an outstanding addition to tomato-based sauces. For the very best dried oregano and other amazing herbs and spices, log on to penzeys.com.

Monday

What I ate:

What I wish I hadn't:

What I did for exercise:

Tuesday

What I ate:

What I wish I hadn't:

What I did for exercise:

Wednesday

What I ate:

What I wish I hadn't:

What I did for exercise:

Thursday

What I ate:

What I wish I hadn't:

What I did for exercise:

Friday

What I ate:

What I wish I hadn't:

What I did for exercise:

Saturday

I REALLY FELT GREAT WHEN I

I CAN GET BETTER AT

NEW FOODS I'M GOING TO TRY

NEXT WEEK I'M GOING TO

GIVE YOURSELF A GRADE
FOR THIS WEEK'S EFFORTS:

What I ate:

What I wish I hadn't:

What I did for exercise:

Sunday

What I ate:

What I wish I hadn't:

What I did for exercise:

Dieting to be skinny is a rail-thin disguise for self-esteem in need of TLC. Skinny doesn't matter. Perfect doesn't exist. You can waste a lot of time trying to deny your genes, or you can work with your doctor and a handpicked team of other trusted professionals, family, and friends to achieve realistic, safe, and healthy results.

kd@chefkathleen.com

SUBJECT: EXERCISE AVOIDANCE DISORDER

FROM: Mary Kay

TO: kd@chefkathleen.com

Dear Kathleen,
I'm being treated for depression and am doing very well. I've heard that exercise can help with moods. The problem is that I don't like to exercise, so when I'm cutting back my list of things to do, it's always the first thing to go.
Mary Kay

REPLY: FEEL-GOOD POTION #9

Dear Mary Kay,
According to the Mayo Clinic, exercise may increase levels of certain mood-enhancing neurotransmitters in the brain and boost feel-good endorphins. It releases muscle tension, diminishes sleep abnormalities, reduces levels of the stress hormone cortisol, and can even increase body temperature, which has calming effects. The best news, according to the report: exercise doesn't have to come in large doses to offer psychological benefits. Even as little as 10 minutes of low-intensity walking helps.

I'm betting that there's nothing else on your to-do list that can deliver the same mood-boosting health benefits. Cross off something else. Create accountability — make an appointment with someone to take nightly walks so that you must show up. Schedule a session with a trainer who will charge you for no-shows. Remember, no one cheers you on when you don't go, but there's usually always someone praising you when you do go. And nothing feels better than a hard-won pat on the back.

Kathleen

FOOD **Throw a pot of water on the stove to boil.** Adding one veggie variety at a time, blanch some green beans, some carrot coins, some bite-size broccoli pieces, and some asparagus spears. Cool completely. Cut asparagus into bite-size pieces. Throw into a large salad bowl. Add some cucumber slices or halved cherry tomatoes and toss with a good bottled dressing or some honey Dijon mustard to which you add balsamic vinegar, olive oil, minced garlic, and dried thyme to taste. Gorge immediately. Store the rest for later.

FUN Write a love letter. Someone in your life needs one: a child, a grandparent, a nephew, a niece, a parent, a sibling, an elderly neighbor. Think of how good you'll both feel when you read it. **Nurture your soul, and it's easier to nurture your body.**

FITNESS When you work out today, think about every single part of your body and all the good you're doing. Think about how exercise benefits your heart, your muscles, your joints, your skin, and your emotions. **Think about the effect a healthy mind and a light heart have on the body.** Think about how a body in good physical shape can troubleshoot unforeseen health conditions a whole lot better than a tired body in bad physical shape running on empty. Think about how nothing is more important than aligning yourself with health and why you can't afford to quit and give up.

FOCUS Negative self-talk produces negative results 100 percent of the time. **Positive self-talk produces positive feelings 100 percent of the time.**

Homework Assignment From Bette Midler's song: "I'm beautiful, I'm beautiful, I'm beautiful, dammit! . . . Become what you were born to be and be it unashamed." Positive thinking breeds positive action. Write down ten positive affirmations—ten things you do excellently. Now make a list of ten things you want to do excellently. Read both lists every day.

YOUR GAME PLAN (STATE YOUR FOOD AND EXERCISE GOALS FOR THE WEEK)

Meaty Bean Fry-Pan Supper

SERVES 6 TO 8 *My neighbor Alice serves this dish to her family all the time. She likes it over noodles, and her kids like to eat it with salsa and sour cream on top, chili-style. I like it served taco-style in warm corn tortillas with extra cilantro sprigs and some diced mango if I'm in the mood.*

½ **pound ground white-meat chicken**

½ **pound lean ground beef**

1 **small onion, finely diced**

1 **garlic clove, minced**

2 **15-ounce cans black beans, rinsed and drained**

1 **teaspoon Tabasco sauce**

1 **teaspoon chili powder**

1 **teaspoon cayenne pepper**

1 **cup loosely packed, coarsely chopped fresh cilantro**

PUT chicken, ground beef, onion, and garlic in a medium skillet and cook on medium heat, stirring often until meats are cooked through and onion is softened, 10 to 15 minutes. Add black beans and enough water to thin to a chili-like consistency, about 3 tablespoons, more or less.

ADD Tabasco sauce, chili powder, and cayenne. Taste and adjust seasonings. Remove from heat, stir in cilantro, and serve.

■ *If you're going to keep this meal around to use throughout the week, skip the cilantro because it doesn't look so hot the next day.*

BEAN COUNTING

Legumes are an excellent source of protein, calcium, and iron.

½ cup serving	Protein	Calcium	Iron
Lentils	9 g	21 ml	3 ml
Navy beans	8 g	64 ml	2 ml
Kidney beans	8 g	25 ml	3 ml
Black beans	8 g	23 ml	2 ml
Pinto beans	7 g	41 ml	2 ml
Black-eyed peas	7 g	19 ml	1 ml
Garbanzo beans	6 g	38 ml	2 ml

One of my favorite I'm-too-tired-to-make-supper last-minute meals: low-sodium, spicy vegetarian refried beans wrapped in a whole-wheat tortilla with ground white-meat chicken, seasoned with chili powder and cumin, with loads of chopped lettuce and salsa fresca.

What I ate:

What I wish I hadn't:

What I did for exercise:

Tuesday

What I ate:

What I wish I hadn't:

What I did for exercise:

Wednesday

What I ate:

What I wish I hadn't:

What I did for exercise:

Thursday

What I ate:

What I wish I hadn't:

What I did for exercise:

Friday

What I ate:

What I wish I hadn't:

What I did for exercise:

REPORT CARD

I REALLY FELT GREAT WHEN I

I CAN GET BETTER AT

NEW FOODS I'M GOING TO TRY

NEXT WEEK I'M GOING TO

GIVE YOURSELF A GRADE
FOR THIS WEEK'S EFFORTS:

Saturday

What I ate:

What I wish I hadn't:

What I did for exercise:

Sunday

What I ate:

What I wish I hadn't:

What I did for exercise:

My friend Miho has cancer. We share the same birthday. We share the same age. Lots of days we share a kitchen and recipes and a whole heap of lessons. Miho can barely speak English. I can't speak a word of Japanese. But when it comes to the tough stuff, we don't need to speak at all. We know that today matters. We know the food we choose to eat can benefit our bodies right now. We know that a restorative walk around the lake after work will do us more good than giving in to depression and defeat. Miho can't quit fighting cancer just because it's scary. I can't quit loving a good friend with cancer just because I'm scared too. And you can't quit eating right or exercising either. Because we all have something to lose. And everything to gain.

kd@chefkathleen.com

SUBJECT: ALL-YOU-CAN-EAT SOUL FOOD BUFFET
FROM: kd@chefkathleen.com
TO: Miho

Dear Miho,
I rode a race this weekend. My first ever. I prefer to ride leisurely distances. I've always been terrified of sprinting. I thought of a hundred ways I could back out, but somehow I made it to the starting line. I immediately thought of how hard you fight and how far you've come. I thought about how honoring my life is the best way I can honor yours. Thank you for teaching me that winners don't quit. My 143rd-place finish made me realize again that I have a lot more to learn. But I know that I can.
    Kathleen

FOOD Practice actively thinking about your fitness, health, and weight-loss goals when you're consuming foods better left uneaten.

FUN Fill the house and your heart with song. **Go to your hi-fi, stereo, boom box, or clock radio and put on some music that moves you.** When was the last time you did that?

FITNESS Protect your lower back: get on the floor in a pushup position. You can rest on your elbows and forearms if it's more comfortable, but push up on your toes. Suck in your abs, tighten, tighten, tighten . . . hold . . . hold . . . breathe . . . go for 15 seconds . . . collapse. Repeat five times.

FOCUS Believing you can achieve something is as essential to your success as the work and follow-through required. **Practice believing until you do.**

Homework Assignment Write down ten things you're deeply thankful for. Describe each thing or person in as much detail as possible. Pretend you get $10 a word. Use your list to help you keep things in perspective, to inspire you to work to your true potential and not give up. Use your list as a reminder that health is everything and that vanity is the first word in the title of a magazine that's fun to read on airplanes.

YOUR GAME PLAN (STATE YOUR FOOD AND EXERCISE GOALS FOR THE WEEK)

Broiled Fish with Lemony Cucumber Yogurt Sauce

SERVES 4 *I encourage you to make this sauce in double batches. It's great with fish or chicken. It's lovely on sandwiches and makes a nice dip for veggies.*

1 **pound white fish, such as tilapia, cod, or grouper**

Coarse salt and cracked black pepper

FOR THE SAUCE

2 **cups low-fat plain yogurt**

1 **tablespoon fresh lemon juice**

1 **teaspoon ground cumin (add $^1/_2$ teaspoon first, taste, and see if you need more)**

1 **medium cucumber, peeled, seeded, and grated or minced**

$^1/_4$ **cup loosely packed, coarsely chopped fresh cilantro**

PREHEAT oven broiler to high. Line broiler pan with foil. Season fish with salt and pepper. In a medium bowl, whisk together yogurt, lemon juice, and cumin. Add cucumber and cilantro. Taste and adjust seasonings with salt and pepper.

PLACE fish skin side down on broiler pan and cook until fork-tender and cooked through, about 4 to 5 minutes per side. Divide among four dinner plates. Serve with yogurt sauce.

THE 5% SOLUTION

According to the National Institutes of Health, if you are overweight, losing as little as 5 percent of your body weight may lower your risk for several diseases, including heart disease and diabetes. If you weigh 200 pounds, this means losing 10 pounds. If you can lose 1 pound, you can lose 10. If you can lose 10, you can lose all the weight you want. Concentrate on losing that first pound by making behavioral changes you can stick with for life.

What I ate:

What I wish I hadn't:

What I did for exercise:

Tuesday

What I ate:

What I wish I hadn't:

What I did for exercise:

Wednesday

What I ate:

What I wish I hadn't:

What I did for exercise:

Thursday

What I ate:

What I wish I hadn't:

What I did for exercise:

Friday

What I ate:

What I wish I hadn't:

What I did for exercise:

REPORT CARD

I REALLY FELT GREAT WHEN I

What I ate:

_____

What I wish I hadn't:

I CAN GET BETTER AT

What I did for exercise:

NEW FOODS I'M GOING TO TRY

What I ate:

_____

NEXT WEEK I'M GOING TO

What I wish I hadn't:

_____

What I did for exercise:

GIVE YOURSELF A GRADE
FOR THIS WEEK'S EFFORTS:

I once worked for an Austrian chef who hated me so much that he tore my glasses from my face and crunched them under his work boots, screaming, "You'll never be anything, Katalin, but a Hausfrau!" I didn't cry in front of him, but I cried. And then I did what I do best: I didn't quit. I worked harder than I ever have until I had enough money to get out of there. He taught me that I didn't have to accept his interpretation of what I could accomplish in life. I'm thankful for my time in his kitchen. I learned to cook, and I learned that no one can facilitate changes in my life but me.

kd@chefkathleen.com

SUBJECT: CLUELESS IN MY KITCHEN

FROM: Chelsea

TO: kd@chefkathleen.com

Dear Kathleen,
I like to cook, but I don't really know what I'm doing. I don't want to be a professional chef, but I want to be more confident in the kitchen and I need to lose weight.

Chelsea

REPLY: READ

Dear Chelsea,
When I was a young culinary student in Judy Rodgers's Zuni Café kitchen in San Francisco, I asked her how I could improve my skills. "Read," she said. "Read cookbooks, Kathleen. Outside of the kitchen, it's the best way to learn about food and cooking."

Some excellent culinary reference books to have on your shelves: *Joy of Cooking* by Irma S. Rombauer, Marion Rombauer Becker, and Ethan Becker; *How to Cook Everything* by Mark Bittman; *Classic Home Desserts* by Richard Sax; *On Food and Cooking* by Harold McGee; *The Zuni Café Cookbook* by Judy Rodgers; *From Julia Child's Kitchen* by Julia Child. Read, Chelsea, read!

Kathleen

FOOD **Cook something new this week,** something you've always wanted to make.

FUN **Read a cookbook.** Pick one for its pure entertainment value or choose one that will help you grow your culinary skills.

FITNESS "I don't exercise because I'm embarrassed about my body, and I don't want anyone to see me" is something I hear a lot. Balls, bells, and the coaches' whistles: fitness toys make working out more fun. **Check out a local sporting goods store for the latest and greatest.** Workout balls are great for stretching, toning, and building core strength. Lightweight dumbbells around the house, especially sets that easily convert from 2 pounds to 25 and up, just might inspire you to work out a little more often. Start by working out at home and in your neighborhood. You may never want to leave home, and that's just fine. This journey is your way or no way!

FOCUS The only way to get good at something is to practice. Practice breeds confidence. **Confidence excites passion.** Practice cooking and exercising until you're passionate about them, or at least passionate about the results!

Homework Assignment

Work to improve your culinary skills this week. To help you decide where to concentrate your energies, make a list of things you "hate" with regard to cooking, then give them the bulk of your time and attention. For instance, if you don't make stir-fries because you always burn them or because the vegetables are never crunchy, tackle stir-fries this week. Google stir-fry recipes and compare them from an ingredient, technique, and equipment standpoint. Open all your cookbooks and do the same. Pick the two recipes that sound the best and make them this week.

YOUR GAME PLAN (STATE YOUR FOOD AND EXERCISE GOALS FOR THE WEEK)

Individual Upside-Down Plum Cakes

MAKES 12 CUPCAKE-SIZE CAKES *Make these cakes with any fruit you like. Raspberries, kiwis, and blueberries work perfectly too. And don't dilly-dally when it comes time to invert the muffins.*

FOR THE FRUIT

- 3 plums, pitted
- 1 tablespoon sugar, or more or less to taste

FOR THE CAKES

- 1¼ cups all-purpose flour
- ½ teaspoon baking soda
- ½ teaspoon salt
- ½ cup granulated sugar
- ½ cup dark brown sugar, packed
- 4 tablespoons (½ stick) unsalted butter, at room temperature
- 1 large egg
- ½ cup low-fat buttermilk
- 1 teaspoon pure vanilla extract

PREHEAT oven to 350°F. Generously spray a nonstick, 12-cup muffin tin with nonstick cooking spray.

FRUIT: Slice plums into thin slices. Slice each slice in half crosswise. Place in a medium bowl. Sprinkle with sugar. Stir occasionally while you prepare batter and mash a little if necessary to break them down.

CAKES: In a medium bowl, sift together flour, baking soda, and salt. In a large bowl, with an electric mixer, cream together sugars and butter until combined. Add egg, buttermilk, and vanilla and mix until completely incorporated. Slowly add dry ingredients to wet, blending thoroughly.

DISTRIBUTE plums evenly among muffin cups. Distribute batter evenly over fruit. Bake for 20 to 25 minutes, or until a toothpick inserted into center of cakes comes out clean. Cool on a wire rack for 10 minutes. Place a large cookie sheet over muffin tin and invert. Serve.

What I ate:

What I wish I hadn't:

What I did for exercise:

Tuesday

What I ate:

What I wish I hadn't:

What I did for exercise:

Wednesday

What I ate:

What I wish I hadn't:

What I did for exercise:

Thursday

What I ate:

What I wish I hadn't:

What I did for exercise:

Friday

What I ate:

What I wish I hadn't:

What I did for exercise:

Saturday

I REALLY FELT GREAT WHEN I

What I ate:

I CAN GET BETTER AT

What I wish I hadn't:

What I did for exercise:

Sunday

NEW FOODS I'M GOING TO TRY

What I ate:

What I wish I hadn't:

NEXT WEEK I'M GOING TO

What I did for exercise:

GIVE YOURSELF A GRADE
FOR THIS WEEK'S EFFORTS:

You can run around *pretending* that you're doing all the right things, or you can do all the right things, make all the right food choices, and exercise enough. If you aren't seeing the results you want, either your goals aren't realistic, you need more time to accomplish them, or you need to step up your game. No one can break down the walls of denial but you. No one can turn kid-yourself internal dialogue into honest self-talk but you. You don't have to go this journey alone, but you do have to initiate all movement and change.

kd@chefkathleen.com

SUBJECT: CARB-STARVED AND DESK-BOUND
FROM: Linda
TO: kd@chefkathleen.com

Dear Kathleen,
I have tried every diet that's out there. The latest was Atkins. But I can't be without my bread and pasta. I need help. I hate figuring out calories. Work is the worst because I am so busy that I eat at my desk. Who has time to count, but how many calories do you think I should eat a day? I think 1200 but am not sure. I weigh a little over 200 pounds and am 5 feet 8½ inches.

Desperate Linda

REPLY: BREAK THE CARB FAST!

Dear Linda,
It's really important to work with your doctor to come up with a calorie count that's safe for your age, height, weight, sex, activity level, and overall health. Focus on the quality and quantity of the food you're consuming and pay attention to calories, but don't obsess. Cut back on junk calories. Obey the voice in your head that lets you know when you're eating the wrong foods or too much food.

Just because you eat at your desk doesn't mean it has to do you in healthwise. Start by cleaning up tomorrow's lunch. Make it healthier. Hold the mayo, add extra veggies, skip the soda, order chicken, order the kid-size fries, bring a healthy lunch from home. The bigger the baby step, the better, *unless* it's so big that you set yourself up to fail.

Kathleen

FOOD Got food? **If I came over for lunch craving bean soup, could you whip up a batch?** If the answer is yes, proceed to the prize palace and pick one. If the answer is no, make things right.

FUN Go to a health food store and buy a whole bunch of canned beans and really cool-looking dried beans. **Nourishing your body nourishes your self-esteem.** Don't worry about what you're going to do with all the beans. That's another day's project. These small wonders of nature are yours for the picking.

FITNESS When you're at the health food store, stock up on whole grains, including whole-grain pastas. **The cleaner your diet is, the more efficiently your body will perform in *and* out of the gym.**

FOCUS What's so hard about making lists? Passing up pink-frosted rainbow-sprinkled circus cookies when my nieces are eating them . . . now that's hard! **Practicing planning is easier than practicing food abstinence.** You can spend your time bogged down with the "bummers" of losing weight, or you can embrace your freedoms and choices and get the job done.

Homework Assignment Pretend you have one day to shop for groceries before a huge snowstorm. Things to stock up on: individual portions of fish to wrap and freeze, ground white-meat chicken to form into patties and freeze, a package of chicken breasts to pound lightly (so they'll cook quicker) and freeze, a pork tenderloin to pound and freeze, a dozen eggs, a gallon of skim milk, lots of whole grains (brown rice, quinoa, oats, and popcorn), low-sodium chicken broth, low-sodium canned and dried beans (lentils, chickpeas, kidney beans, pinto beans, and any other kind of bean that looks good). Also: prewashed baby greens, prewashed baby spinach, and pregrated carrots for easy salads. Buy long-lasting veggies such as broccoli, asparagus, cauliflower, green beans, and hard winter squash, sweet potatoes, an onion or two, and a head of garlic. Enough ingredients to mix, match, and make at least twenty meals!

YOUR GAME PLAN (STATE YOUR FOOD AND EXERCISE GOALS FOR THE WEEK)

Creamy Asian Chicken Salad

SERVES 4 *This hit-the-spot salad is great when it's too hot to cook. It can be as dump-and-go-easy as you want to make it. I try to work in as many extra veggies as I can so I'm not tempted to eat a huge heaping bowl of ice cream for dessert.*

½ **pound boneless, skinless chicken breast**

⅓ **cup creamy peanut butter**

3 **tablespoons rice wine vinegar**

½ **teaspoon sesame oil**

8 **cups washed torn garden lettuces**

1½ **cups grated carrots (half a 10-ounce bag)**

1 **red, yellow, or orange bell pepper, seeded and very thinly sliced**

IN a small pot or skillet, place chicken breast and enough water to cover. Poach chicken over medium-high heat until just cooked, 6 to 8 minutes. Let chicken cool, then shred into thin pieces.

MEANWHILE, in a microwave-proof bowl that you'll serve the salad in, place peanut butter and ⅓ cup water. Microwave on high for 7 to 10 seconds, or just until peanut butter is soft enough to whisk together with water. Add rice wine vinegar and sesame oil and whisk until combined. Add lettuces, carrots, bell pepper, and cooked chicken to bowl, toss until completely coated, and serve.

SESAME OIL

Light sesame oil is cold-pressed from raw seeds, making it pale in color and light in flavor. Dark sesame oil is pressed from hulled, toasted seeds, creating a richer, denser oil with a more full-bodied, intensely nutty flavor and making it the preferred choice for Asian cooking.

For a show-stopping side dish, toss leftover cooked green beans with a teaspoon or so of sesame oil in a non-stick pan and cook over medium heat until hot, then sprinkle with rice vinegar and a pinch of white or black sesame seeds.

Monday

What I ate:

What I wish I hadn't:

What I did for exercise:

Tuesday

What I ate:

What I wish I hadn't:

What I did for exercise:

Wednesday

What I ate:

What I wish I hadn't:

What I did for exercise:

Thursday

What I ate:

What I wish I hadn't:

What I did for exercise:

Friday

What I ate:

What I wish I hadn't:

What I did for exercise:

REPORT CARD

I REALLY FELT GREAT WHEN I

I CAN GET BETTER AT

NEW FOODS I'M GOING TO TRY

NEXT WEEK I'M GOING TO

GIVE YOURSELF A GRADE
FOR THIS WEEK'S EFFORTS:

Saturday

What I ate:

What I wish I hadn't:

What I did for exercise:

Sunday

What I ate:

What I wish I hadn't:

What I did for exercise:

Try the sleep diet. "Sleep loss is associated with striking alterations in hormone levels that may contribute to obesity," says Michael Thorpy, M.D., director of the Sleep-Wake Disorders Center at Montefiore Medical Center in New York. "If you want to lose weight, get more sleep."

kd@chefkathleen.com

SUBJECT: NIGHT HOWL
FROM: Elizabeth
TO: kd@chefkathleen.com

Dear Kathleen,
My life is out of control. So's my weight. Work is stressful, and then I come home and have to deal with the kids and housework until it's time to go to bed. My husband helps some, but he works late a lot. You would think I'd be tired, but sometimes I lay there and stress out until morning. We eat a lot of carryout and bad food. I feel guilty. Help!
Elizabeth

REPLY: THROW A PAJAMA PARTY!

Dear Elizabeth,
Pretend your life is a Key lime pie. Cut it into eighths and tackle a wedge at a time. Scrutinize breakfast, lunch, dinner, house duties, date nights, sleep rituals, spousal support, time off.

List things you can do that will enable you to feel more in control. Under breakfast, lunch, and dinner, list easy meals you can get on the table in a reasonable amount of time. They don't all have to be from scratch.

Make a list of daily chores, split them up over the week, and see how much you can assign to other family members. Weigh the cost of hiring a housekeeper once a month. Sit down with your husband and carve out four date nights a month. Make a list of peaceful, calming things you can do before bedtime to help you wind down. Get the kids into PJs early. Put yours on at the same time. Pull down the shades and turn off the lights earlier than normal. Turn off all TVs an hour before bedtime. As you work your way through the lists, you will regain control. Seek support when you need it so that you don't feel alone.

Kathleen

FOOD Curl up with a good book and a cozy dessert. Take a baked, grilled, or broiled halved plum (minus the pit) and mound with peach sorbet and fresh raspberries.

FUN Is your bed fun to sleep in? Are your sheets cozy? Is the room inviting? Is it time to use up all the Bed Bath & Beyond coupons you've been hoarding? They accept expired ones, you know.

FITNESS Feel-good endorphins released during exercise can affect your ability to get a good night's sleep. You might feel too jazzed and energized to wind down at a decent hour so try to get your workout in at least three hours before bedtime.

FOCUS Sleep is as important to weight loss and good health as eating and exercise.

Homework Assignment Apply Elizabeth's homework to your own life. Get started today. When one area is too tough to deal with, skip to something else. The only rule: cross something off your list each and every day. You're either making lists, brainstorming solutions, or you're making change. Anything is better than nothing. Action is the only path to resolution.

YOUR GAME PLAN (STATE YOUR FOOD AND EXERCISE GOALS FOR THE WEEK)

Spicy Oven-Roasted Chickpeas

SERVES 4 *I'm forever trying to come up with ways of re-creating some of my favorite deep-fried foods. These roasted chickpeas are really great when you're in the mood for something deep-fried and salty minus the calories.*

1 **19-ounce can chickpeas, drained, rinsed, and patted dry**
Olive oil spray
Coarse salt to taste
1/8 **teaspoon cayenne pepper, or more to taste**
1/8 **teaspoon garlic powder, or more to taste**
1/4 **teaspoon dried oregano, or more to taste**

PREHEAT oven to 450°F. Pour chickpeas onto a rimmed cookie sheet.

BAKE, shaking every now and then, until golden brown and crunchy, 35 to 40 minutes.

POUR into a large bowl. Lightly coat with olive oil spray. Add salt, cayenne, garlic powder, and oregano. Toss to coat evenly. Serve.

GRAB A GARBANZO

Chickpeas (also called garbanzo beans) are a high-protein (5 grams per ½-cup serving) complex-carbohydrate, rich-in-cholesterol-lowering soluble fiber, the kind of fiber that leaves you feeling full and satisfied. They're also high in potassium, which may help reduce blood pressure.

3 Easy Ways to Work Chickpeas into Your Diet

1. Add drained and rinsed chickpeas to salads.

2. Make the Sausage, Chickpea, and Sweet Potato Stew in Week 34 and freeze the leftovers for meals later.

3. Keep hummus in your fridge next to a stash of baby carrots, tiny tomatoes, celery sticks, and radishes for "chip" and dip emergencies.

Monday

What I ate:

What I wish I hadn't:

What I did for exercise:

Tuesday

What I ate:

What I wish I hadn't:

What I did for exercise:

Wednesday

What I ate:

What I wish I hadn't:

What I did for exercise:

Thursday

What I ate:

What I wish I hadn't:

What I did for exercise:

Friday

What I ate:

What I wish I hadn't:

What I did for exercise:

Saturday

I REALLY FELT GREAT WHEN I

I CAN GET BETTER AT

NEW FOODS I'M GOING TO TRY

NEXT WEEK I'M GOING TO

GIVE YOURSELF A GRADE
FOR THIS WEEK'S EFFORTS:

What I ate:

What I wish I hadn't:

What I did for exercise:

Sunday

What I ate:

What I wish I hadn't:

What I did for exercise:

Big, Bad Habit–Exchange Bingo

It takes four months before a tomato grown from seed is ready to make its salad bowl debut. "Buns" are in the oven for nine months. And it takes fourteen years of hard work to graduate from high school. Losing weight takes time too. Instead of thinking of this as a diet (it is not), think of it as the Big, Bad-Habit Exchange. All you have to do is show up every Monday ready to trade up again.

kd@chefkathleen.com

SUBJECT: I WROTE THE I-HATE-TO-COOK BOOK

FROM: Tabitha
TO: kd@chefkathleen.com

Dear Kathleen,
My doctor told me to lose weight or risk having a heart attack. I have lost 30 pounds by skipping meals and drinking lots of diet soda. I know this is bad, but I hate to cook.

Tabitha

REPLY: HEALTHY IN A HURRY

Dear Tabitha,
It's certainly harder to eat healthy foods if you won't cook, but it's not impossible. I'm guessing you used to drop at least $15 a day on fast food. Take that money and spend it on fast health food. Visit all the grocery stores in your area and check out their gourmet-to-go sections. Pick up restaurant takeout menus every chance you get. You can look up a lot of menus online. Explore the possibility of having meals delivered for the week. Figure out who has healthy options that appeal to you. Program their phone numbers into your phone and call them before you leave work so dinner is ready for you on the way home. Check out frozen dinners too, but pay attention to the labels with an eye toward overall quality and quantity of calories, total nutrition, and sodium.

Kathleen

FOOD **You choose:** a high-calorie cereal bar that doesn't fill you up or the Pesto Primavera Microwave Frittata in Week 32.

FUN **Time off from everything brings clarity and peace.** Get to know your local parks, plant 100 bulbs in your garden, hunt for seashells, follow a butterfly, or get a new bird feeder and hang it where you take your morning tea.

FITNESS Instead of skipping your exercise on days you're "not in the mood," do something more appealing. **Run an errand that will require you to hoof it a bit, such as shopping in a giant mall.**

FOCUS **Taking the focus off dieting and deprivation opens the door for manageable positive change.**

Homework Assignment

Tackle and upgrade one habit at a time. For example, if your candy bar habit is sabotaging your weight-loss efforts, make a list of the upgrade possibilities:

* Switch to a lower-calorie candy bar.

* Switch to pretzels.

* Switch to a lower-calorie granola bar with a better nutritional makeup.

* Switch to a serving of whole-grain cereal, a serving of fruit, or a serving of vegetables.

YOUR GAME PLAN (STATE YOUR FOOD AND EXERCISE GOALS FOR THE WEEK)

Chicken and Crunchy Potato Salad

SERVES 6 TO 8 *This Asian-inspired version is a great alternative to your regular picnic-style potato salad. Julienned veggies and chicken are lightly cooked, and the potatoes retain a delightful coleslaw crunch. It's great slightly warm and excellent the next day out of the refrigerator.*

1½ **cups grated carrots (about half a bag)**

½ **pound boneless, skinless chicken breast, pounded, thinly sliced**

1 **large red potato, peeled and julienned into 2-inch-long, ⅛-inch-wide strips**

1 **small onion, very thinly sliced**

3 **celery stalks (about 5 ounces), thinly sliced**

2 **cups chopped fresh basil**

½ **cup white wine vinegar or champagne vinegar**

1 **garlic clove, grated**

½ **cup grated Parmesan cheese**
Coarse salt and cracked black pepper

BRING 2 quarts water in a medium saucepan to a boil. Add carrots and cook for about 1 minute. Add chicken and boil for 3 to 5 minutes until all chicken turns white.

ADD potato and onion to boiling water and cook for about 30 seconds. Drain and rinse with cold water until cooled. Drain any excess water, then add celery and basil.

TOSS vegetables and cooked chicken together in a large bowl with vinegar, garlic, and Parmesan. Add salt and pepper to taste and serve.

ANOTHER REASON TO EAT YOUR BROCCOLI

According to the National Cancer Institute, American women who eat the most fruit, vegetables, or fruit and vegetables combined have a 21 to 32 percent lower risk of lung cancer. Lung cancer risk is considerably higher among women who consume fewer than two servings of fruits and vegetables a day. Cruciferous vegetables (broccoli, cauliflower, Brussels sprouts, cabbage), citrus fruits, and fruits and vegetables high in total carotenoids (yellow and red ones) give the most protection.

Monday

What I ate:

What I wish I hadn't:

What I did for exercise:

Tuesday

What I ate:

What I wish I hadn't:

What I did for exercise:

Wednesday

What I ate:

What I wish I hadn't:

What I did for exercise:

Thursday

What I ate:

What I wish I hadn't:

What I did for exercise:

Friday

What I ate:

What I wish I hadn't:

What I did for exercise:

Saturday

I REALLY FELT GREAT WHEN I

What I ate:

I CAN GET BETTER AT

What I wish I hadn't:

What I did for exercise:

NEW FOODS I'M GOING TO TRY

Sunday

What I ate.

What I wish I hadn't:

NEXT WEEK I'M GOING TO

What I did for exercise:

GIVE YOURSELF A GRADE
FOR THIS WEEK'S EFFORTS:

Research shows that we consume up to 1000 calories more when we dine out. I'd hate to see a study on how many excess calories we eat when we're wearing our fat pants. Don't tell me you don't have at least one pair, Pinocchio. If this is you, throw them away. And when you're feeling bingey, put on your tightest pair. Nothing curbs your appetite quicker than an inability to breathe between bites.

kd@chefkathleen.com

SUBJECT: FROG PRINCESS
FROM: Lesley
TO: kd@chefkathleen.com

Dear Kathleen,
I'm really frustrated with trying to lose weight. I'm fat and ugly in clothes.
  Lesley

REPLY: EXTREME MAKEOVER, DIVA EDITION

Dear Lesley,
I'm no looker first thing in the morning either. It takes hours of face putty, hot rollers, and wardrobe anxiety to get answer-the-door respectable.

Clothes don't make the woman, but they can make you feel pretty darn good. Go through your wardrobe and pick out all the stuff that makes you feel "fat and ugly." Fold it up nicely and store it far away in the basement or the garage with a note to donate it to an organization in need of clothing. Pay attention to how you feel during this exercise.

Next, go through your wardrobe and pick out everything that makes you feel really good and happy. No pouting. If there's only one outfit, you get to go shopping. But until you do, wear your pretty clothes every day. You aren't dressing to please anyone but yourself.

  Kathleen

FOOD **If your proportion of fat-pants food to tight-jeans cuisine is off, do something about it.** Right now. As in today. Romaine lettuces, basil, mint, cilantro, grated carrots, a can of white albacore tuna, and low-calorie sesame miso dressing is lean like the jeans you'll soon be sliding into!

FUN Play dress up. **Plan your outfits for the upcoming week.** Dress for success. Accessorize! Handbags for every outfit.

FITNESS Do you feel good in your fitness clothes? If not, why not? You deserve to feel fresh, sexy, and in your element every single day. No one can give you that confidence but you. **A fitness wardrobe you like is the first step.** Mirror, mirror on the wall, *I'm* the fairest of them all is step two. Say it every time you look in the mirror. You heard me. It's free, it's true, and even if you don't believe it yet, with practice, you will soon enough. Don't make me stand next to you.

FOCUS Just because you're not in the mood to deal with eating right or exercise doesn't mean you get to "waste" a day. Your kids can't stay home from school when they don't feel like going. They're watching everything you do. **Off to your workout!**

Homework Assignment Go through your closet like Cojo is on his way over to bust you for wardrobe violations on national television. Get rid of all your aiding-and-abetting clothes. If they don't make you feel positive, productive, and happy, get rid of them or take them down to the basement and store them near the paint. You can wear gross clothes to paint in and that's it.

YOUR GAME PLAN (STATE YOUR FOOD AND EXERCISE GOALS FOR THE WEEK)

Eggplant with Ginger, Garlic, and Soy

SERVES 4 *It doesn't really matter what kind of eggplant you use, but this recipe is really nice with the smallest kind you can find, such as Japanese or baby eggplant, which it's not necessary to peel.*

- 2 **tablespoons soy sauce**
- 2 **tablespoons chicken broth**
- 1 **tablespoon mirin**
- 1 **teaspoon sesame oil**
- 1 **tablespoon minced fresh ginger**
- 1 **pound eggplant, peeled, sliced lengthwise, and then cut into ½-inch-thick slices**
- 2 **garlic cloves, very thinly sliced**
- 2 **scallions, white and green parts, very thinly sliced**

IN a small bowl, whisk together soy sauce, chicken broth, mirin, sesame oil, and ginger.

PLACE eggplant on a large plate in a single layer (if you have to pile a few slices on top of one another, don't worry; the recipe will work fine). Sprinkle garlic and scallions evenly over eggplant. Pour marinade over eggplant. Cover tightly with plastic wrap and place in microwave. Cook on high for 4 minutes. Let stand for 5 minutes. Remove plastic and serve.

■ *Mirin, a Japanese rice wine, is available in the Asian section of gourmet grocery stores.*

GOOD EGGS

Look for blemish-free, smooth-skinned, firm eggplants. Mushy with scabs, you don't want. Whenever I come upon a new eggplant variety, I plug it into my regular eggplant recipes. Japanese eggplants, which are sold in the Asian section of gourmet produce markets, have thinner skins than regular eggplants and fewer seeds.

If you somehow end up with more eggplants than any one person should have in the fridge, peel them, slice them into ¼-inch-thick rounds, layer them onto a large microwave-safe dinner plate, cover loosely with plastic wrap, and cook on high for 5 minutes, or until completely soft. Season them with salt and pepper, place in a refrigerator dish, and douse them with great balsamic vinegar. They keep for about a week. Eat them right out of the container, on sandwiches and in salads. Yum!

Monday

What I ate:

What I wish I hadn't:

What I did for exercise:

Tuesday

What I ate:

What I wish I hadn't:

What I did for exercise:

Wednesday

What I ate:

What I wish I hadn't:

What I did for exercise:

Thursday

What I ate:

What I wish I hadn't:

What I did for exercise:

Friday

What I ate:

What I wish I hadn't:

What I did for exercise:

REPORT CARD

Saturday

I REALLY FELT GREAT WHEN I

I CAN GET BETTER AT

NEW FOODS I'M GOING TO TRY

NEXT WEEK I'M GOING TO

GIVE YOURSELF A GRADE
FOR THIS WEEK'S EFFORTS:

What I ate:

What I wish I hadn't:

What I did for exercise:

Sunday

What I ate:

What I wish I hadn't:

What I did for exercise:

Got lipstick? Cake without icing is dull. Because it's cheaper than an hour on the therapist's couch, I wear makeup almost every day. When I don't feel good or am the slightest bit pity-poor-me, I spackle the makeup on thicker than a painter trying to get away with one coat. It makes me feel better than staring back at that weathered bag lady with the same Social Security number as mine. When I dress like a pro, I eat like a pro, and I exercise like a pro. And then I feel like a pro.

kd@chefkathleen.com

SUBJECT: FREIDA FRUMP-ITIS
FROM: Jackie
TO: kd@chefkathleen.com

Dear Kathleen,
My daughter asked why I don't wear lipstick "like all the other moms do." I don't remember what excuse I came up with, but I realized that she was probably noticing that I'm not as put-together as the other moms. I don't even know where to start.

Jackie

REPLY: CINDERELLA, TO THE BALL!

Dear Jackie,
Makeup counters are a great place to start. Most reps offer a free application. Before you go, rip out pictures in magazines of people whose makeup or look you admire and take them with you when you go. Research different lines through friends and by reading about products online. And then head to the mall and visit the various counters. If you're concerned about feeling pressure to buy, eavesdrop on clerk-customer conversations until you feel comfortable with a particular rep. Explain that you're on a fact-finding mission to learn about different products and what will work for your skin type and budget. It's perfectly reasonable to let the makeup artists know you'd like to think about what makes sense for you to purchase. These guys are professionals. I've found that most of them don't use pressure tactics. Have fun, Jackie!

Kathleen

FOOD **What do you suppose your role models eat for power lunches every day?** Which would you rather your boss's boss saw you eating—chili cheese fries and a Diet Coke or a grilled chicken salad and a bottle of water?

FUN **Plan a girls' night out at a department store makeup counter.**

FITNESS Why shouldn't you feel cute and sexy at the gym? **Accessorize your gym wardrobe: baseball caps and cute socks make great rewards.**

FOCUS It's not how you look, it's how you *feel*. You are the only person in the whole world who can make *you* feel happy. **If you want to turn gray skies sunny, think about someone in your life who brings a giant smile to your heart.** And let the thought flow till you're smiling on the outside.

Homework Assignment Figure out what combination of clothing and grooming makes you feel the best and work to achieve that look and feel every day. *Even* on the weekends! The only day you can wear fat pants is the day after Thanksgiving. Got it? That's if you want to waste your whole day lollygagging about when you could be burning perfectly useless calories by shopping like crazy or playing touch football or enjoying a brisk fall walk through crunchy, colorful leaves.

YOUR GAME PLAN (STATE YOUR FOOD AND EXERCISE GOALS FOR THE WEEK)

Black Bean, Corn, Tomato, and Avocado Salsa

SERVES 6 TO 8 *This dish is fabulous as a quickie salad. Or use it to dress up plain grilled chicken, fish, or seared steak.*

2 **large tomatoes, cored, peeled, and diced**

1 **15-ounce can black beans, drained and rinsed**

1 **cup fresh corn kernels (about 2 ears)**

1 **ripe avocado, peeled, pitted, and diced**

1 **tablespoon grated jalapeño pepper**

2 **tablespoons fresh lime juice**

2 **tablespoons balsamic vinegar**

1/2 **cup loosely packed, coarsely chopped fresh cilantro**

Coarse salt to taste

PLACE all ingredients in a bowl. Toss until combined. Taste and adjust seasonings. Serve.

STAY AS SWEET AS YOU ARE

Supersweet varieties of corn contain about twice the sugar of traditional sweet corn. Their texture is generally crisper. But their real advantage is that their sugars take much longer to convert to starch, so the kernels stay sweet and crunchy for days, while those of ordinary corn become starchy within twenty-four hours. This staying power is ideal for a crop that may need to be shipped all the way across the country to distant markets.

If you've never had a salad of raw sweet corn, put it on your culinary to-do list. The very next time you can get sweet and tender young corn, cut off the cob, toss with champagne vinegar, extra-virgin olive oil, and season with salt and pepper to taste. Add anything else special you have in the fridge: leftover roasted beets, heirloom tomatoes, or blanched green beans. What do you mean your fridge isn't stocked with such edible treasures? We're in Week 43 already!

Monday

What I ate:

What I wish I hadn't:

What I did for exercise:

Tuesday

What I ate:

What I wish I hadn't:

What I did for exercise:

Wednesday

What I ate:

What I wish I hadn't:

What I did for exercise:

Thursday

What I ate:

What I wish I hadn't:

What I did for exercise:

Friday

What I ate:

What I wish I hadn't:

What I did for exercise:

REPORT CARD

Saturday

I REALLY FELT GREAT WHEN I

What I ate:

What I wish I hadn't:

I CAN GET BETTER AT

What I did for exercise:

Sunday

NEW FOODS I'M GOING TO TRY

What I ate:

NEXT WEEK I'M GOING TO

What I wish I hadn't:

What I did for exercise:

GIVE YOURSELF A GRADE
FOR THIS WEEK'S EFFORTS:

Nope. You're a permanent resident on Temptation Island. I've maintained a 75-pound weight loss for over twelve years, give or take the winter 5 pounds that creep on as I move less. They mysteriously shed in summers when I'm magically motivated to go outside and play more. If I thought for a single minute I was on any kind of a diet, I would have quit long ago. You're in the driver's seat too. No speeding. Keep your eyes on the road ahead of you and be safe out there.

kd@chefkathleen.com

SUBJECT: I'M IN DIET JAIL!
FROM: Carrie
TO: kd@chefkathleen.com

Dear Kathleen,
I feel as if I've been sentenced to life in diet prison. I've been on a diet all my life because I've been on one ever since I can remember. I am sick of being heavy. I fill up my cart with everything "healthy," but then I do something like throw in a bag of cookies or a half gallon of ice cream and eat it all myself. Half the healthy stuff I buy goes to waste because I get busy and then I eat out. Help!
   Carrie

REPLY: FREE YOURSELF!

Dear Carrie,
Feeling like you're on a diet all the time is like carrying around a real-life ball and chain. This week, earn the privilege of eating out (healthy, of course). Instead of filling up your cart with healthy stuff, find three *easy* recipes that appeal to you and buy the ingredients to prepare them. Increase the number of nights you cook at home. As you increase the number of nights you cook in, increase your rewards to keep things fun. Instead of putting a whole bag of cookies or a half gallon of ice cream in your cart, buy a single cookie or pastry from the bakery department instead. Do not bring more than one serving of treats into the house at a time. I promise you, if you stick to the rules, you'll consume fewer calories. You can do this, Carrie!
   Kathleen

FOOD Figure out the number of calories in one of your favorite "treat" foods and then figure out how much exercise you'll need to do to burn it off. **Fitday.com and caloriesperhour.com are free online resources.** One of my favorite snacks is veil-thin slices of prosciutto wrapped around thick slices of perfectly ripe melon. The butcher will cut the prosciutto any way you like. Don't order more than 2 ounces, and you won't eat more than 2 ounces.

FUN Plan a girls' night out, even if it's with only one friend. **Plan an evening start to finish around things you love to do, and keep it healthy.** Sushi and bowling, a power walk in the park, and a picnic dinner and a movie (sneak in your own popcorn: I do it all the time, don't *care* if it's tacky).

FITNESS **If you have time to go out and eat, to shop, to watch TV, to gab on the phone, to surf the Net, you have time to exercise.** Cut something else out but don't slack here or you'll never have enough room in your pants for your legs or in your diet for treats.

FOCUS **You don't have to like eating healthy and you don't have to want to exercise.** You just have to do both if you want to preserve and protect your health.

Homework Assignment Write down the top 10 things you "hate" about this whole process. Then pretend they're my gripes. Give me a written game plan. Teach me how to see things more positively and how to approach things more realistically. Send it to me at kd@chefkathleen.com. You just might see it in a future book with your name on it and a great big thank-you!

YOUR GAME PLAN (STATE YOUR FOOD AND EXERCISE GOALS FOR THE WEEK)

Commuter Supper: Summer Squash, Basil, and Parmesan Frittata

SERVES 4 *You can whip up this supper from start to finish in fifteen minutes, and the leftovers are heavenly. I like to use fresh eggs, but any egg substitute will work just fine.*

8 **large egg whites**

2 **large eggs**

Coarse salt and cracked black pepper

2 **teaspoons olive oil**

3 **garlic cloves, very thinly sliced**

2 **medium summer squashes, thinly sliced (about 1 pound)**

1 **cup loosely packed, coarsely chopped fresh basil**

About ½ cup grated Parmesan cheese (½ ounce)

PREHEAT broiler. Whisk egg whites and eggs together in a large bowl. Season with salt and pepper. Set aside.

PLACE oil and garlic in a 10-inch nonstick skillet with an ovenproof handle. Turn heat to medium and cook until garlic just starts to sizzle. Add squash and cook, stirring every now and then, until garlic is lightly golden and squash is cooked through, 5 to 6 minutes. Season with salt and pepper to taste.

POUR egg mixture into pan and add basil. Using a heat-proof spatula, slowly stir eggs in a figure-eight motion until just beginning to set on edges. Continue cooking, occasionally sliding spatula around edges of pan to let raw egg flow underneath, until frittata is set on bottom but not all the way on top, 4 to 5 minutes.

SCATTER Parmesan over frittata and place pan directly under broiler just until top is golden brown and set and cheese has melted, 1 to 2 minutes. Let frittata stand for 5 to 10 minutes. To serve, slide frittata onto a serving platter and cut into wedges. Frittata may also be cooled to room temperature, then cut and served.

THE REAL TRUTH ABOUT EGGS

The *Journal of the American Medical Association* reports on a study by the Harvard School of Public Health that found no relationship between egg consumption and cardiovascular disease in a population of more than 117,000 nurses and health professionals followed for eight to fourteen years. There was no difference in risk between those who ate less than one egg a week and those who ate more than one.

Bottom line: there's no reason eggs can't be part of a naturally healthy diet . . . but load up your plate of eggs with bacon, sausage, flapjacks, syrup, and butter, and you'll reap what you sow.

My very favorite egg book? *Country Egg, City Egg* by Gayle Pirie and John Clark, chefowners of San Francisco's superswank Mission District eatery, Foreign Cinema.

Monday

What I ate:

What I wish I hadn't:

What I did for exercise:

Tuesday

What I ate:

What I wish I hadn't:

What I did for exercise:

Wednesday

What I ate:

What I wish I hadn't:

What I did for exercise:

Thursday

What I ate:

What I wish I hadn't:

What I did for exercise:

Friday

What I ate:

What I wish I hadn't:

What I did for exercise:

REPORT CARD

I REALLY FELT GREAT WHEN I

I CAN GET BETTER AT

NEW FOODS I'M GOING TO TRY

NEXT WEEK I'M GOING TO

GIVE YOURSELF A GRADE
FOR THIS WEEK'S EFFORTS:

Saturday

What I ate:

What I wish I hadn't:

What I did for exercise:

Sunday

What I ate:

What I wish I hadn't:

What I did for exercise:

Self-imposed roadblocks are a signal to regroup. Hear yourself as others hear you. "No time for breakfast" is a choice. "No time for exercise" is a choice. "No time to cook" is a choice. "No time for myself" is a choice. I'm not saying it's easy to make the right choices, but it's something you need to do. If you're not seeing progress where progress is possible, you're not doing everything possible to achieve it.

kd@chefkathleen.com

SUBJECT: MY MOM'S A FRY-MONSTER!

FROM: Maria

TO: kd@chefkathleen.com

Dear Kathleen,
Everyone in my family is heavy. I am sixteen years old, and my "baby fat" hasn't gone away. My family eats all of the wrong foods, but my mother and grandmother do all the cooking. They deep-fry many dishes. I weigh 200 pounds. I don't like feeling different.
*   Maria*

REPLY: TAKE MATTERS INTO YOUR HANDS

Dear Maria,
Here are some things you can do:

1. Have a salad at dinner every night so there's something for you after you have a portion of the main dish.

2. Try to avoid sugary sodas, chips, candy, donuts, and other junk food. If your friends are having pizza, order a salad and have one or two slices of pizza instead of three or four.

3. Here's where you can do the most work to lose weight right now: try to exercise at least thirty minutes a day, five times a week. Go for fast walks.

4. Seek out support. Find someone you can talk to. Start a weight-loss blog for teens. Find an exercise buddy.

    Best wishes for great health, Maria! You can do this!
    Kathleen

FOOD Button things up this week. Do a mental rundown of the contents in your cupboards right now. **What's sabotaging you the most?** Challenge yourself to get rid of it. Here are a few of my favorite snacks: cheese and crackers—without the cheese and crackers. Instead, prepare carrot "crackers" by slicing a peeled carrot in half crosswise and cutting each half into slices lengthwise and then into soda cracker size. Use the slices (from the bottom) as the crackers and the narrower slices (top half) to dip. Or use cucumber or radish slices, or Belgian endive leaves in place of crackers. Try rich toppings, such as red pepper puree, hummus, tabbouleh, baba ghanoush, or lemony goat cheese spread.

FUN **Splurge on a dozen farm-fresh eggs or some food item that's healthy and decadent:** a live lobster, king crab, sea scallops, or organic anything that you don't normally indulge in.

FITNESS **Your body will achieve what your mind directs it to.** If you think you can increase the intensity of your workouts, you can. If you tell yourself you're "tired," you will achieve tired results.

FOCUS Exercise choice. **Choose to succeed, and you will.**

Homework Assignment Make a list of all the excuses Now Playing in your head: I'm too tired, I don't *feel* like cooking, I'm a picky eater, I *do* work out, I *deserve* to have this, a little won't hurt, one day off won't kill me, yada yada. Next to each excuse, write down something your inner goddess of success would say. For example: I'm too tired, but I will feel so much better mentally after a good workout. I will feel proud of myself for getting through it. It's the right thing to do, and I need to set an example for my family. I'm going to work out and I'm going to give it everything I have.

YOUR GAME PLAN (STATE YOUR FOOD AND EXERCISE GOALS FOR THE WEEK)

Warm Wild Rice Salad with Blue Cheese, Pears, Apples, and Toasted Walnuts

SERVES 4 TO 6 *You can garnish the lettuce leaves of this salad with thin slices of red-skinned or any ripe pears. Serve with 8 to 12 ounces of very thinly sliced pan-seared boneless, skinless chicken breast.*

- 1 **cup mixed brown and wild rice**
- 1 **pear, peeled, cored, and cut into bite-size pieces**
- 1 **apple, peeled, cored, and cut into bite-size pieces**
- ¼ **cup toasted walnuts, chopped**
- 2 **ounces Maytag Blue cheese, crumbled**
- ⅓ **cup dried cranberries**
  Coarse salt and cracked black pepper
- 8 **cups washed torn salad greens**
- 1 **tablespoon olive oil**
- 2 **teaspoons champagne vinegar or red wine vinegar**

COOK rice in a large pot of boiling water until tender and cooked through, 30 to 35 minutes. Drain and return to pot. Add pear, apple, walnuts, cheese, and cranberries. Taste and adjust seasonings with salt and pepper.

PLACE salad greens in a large mixing bowl. Add olive oil and vinegar. Toss to coat evenly. Taste and adjust seasonings with salt and pepper. Divide among serving plates. Distribute rice evenly over each salad and serve.

■ *To toast walnuts, place in a nonstick pan over medium heat and cook, stirring occasionally, until fragrant and toasted, about 5 minutes. Be sure to watch them carefully or they might burn.*

WORDS FOR THE COOK-WEARY

Weight-loss success story Alli says: "Turn your own kitchen into your favorite restaurant. Print and post your Weekly Specials Menu on the fridge. Fill the menu with healthy, easy, and fast meals and fill your fridge with healthy, tasty, and easy snacks. With the right attitude, you can have your own personal spa chef—you!"

What I ate:

What I wish I hadn't:

What I did for exercise:

What I ate:

What I wish I hadn't:

What I did for exercise:

Wednesday

What I ate:

What I wish I hadn't:

What I did for exercise:

Thursday

What I ate:

What I wish I hadn't:

What I did for exercise:

Friday

What I ate:

What I wish I hadn't:

What I did for exercise:

REPORT CARD

Saturday

I REALLY FELT GREAT WHEN I

What I ate:

What I wish I hadn't:

I CAN GET BETTER AT

What I did for exercise:

NEW FOODS I'M GOING TO TRY

Sunday

What I ate:

What I wish I hadn't:

NEXT WEEK I'M GOING TO

What I did for exercise:

GIVE YOURSELF A GRADE
FOR THIS WEEK'S EFFORTS:

Help! My Family Is Making Me Fat!

It doesn't matter how you ended up with a family whose eating habits are less than healthy. The only thing that's important now is that you make a decision to turn things around. Don't go boot-camp crazy. But at the next family meal, announce the culinary about-face. Ask everyone for cooperation and input. Start introducing new foods. Be consistent with your actions and resistant to objections. The others'll stop complaining sooner or later.

kd@chefkathleen.com

SUBJECT: FOOD FIGHTS
FROM: Charlotte
TO: kd@chefkathleen.com

Dear Kathleen,
I love veggies, but my family is something else. My husband is a meat-and-potatoes man. He will eat lettuce, green beans, and peas. One of my boys likes asparagus. The other hates it. One likes Brussels sprouts. The other hates them. I can get one to eat raw carrots and the other to eat cooked. I don't want to fix two or three meals at night—I barely have the energy to fix one. How do I lose weight?
    Charlotte

REPLY: THE SHORT-ORDER COOK QUIT

Dear Charlotte,
If your husband is fit and healthy and wants meat and potatoes, there's a healthy way to prepare meat-and-potato meals. Portion control is key. Serve plenty of vegetable sides and or a large salad. Leading by example is the very best gift you can give everyone. Try this three-pronged approach:

  1. Protein—meat, chicken, or fish, grilled or broiled

  2. Salad—serve at every meal so there's always something for you to fill up on. Wash the lettuces in batches so you don't have to do it every night. Use the prepped ingredients in the markets: grated carrots, broccoli slaw, sprouts, baby spinach, cherry tomatoes.

  3. Veggie sides—one or two a night—keep 'em simple. Microwave or roast large batches of vegetables at a time. Your family will come around eventually if you don't budge.
    Kathleen

FOOD Ask your family to give you a list of healthy foods they like. Remind them that french fries do *not* count as a vegetable. Start building your weekly menus with as many good ingredients as you can. Once everyone gets used to the program, get creative. Expand the offerings to include more healthy foods by modifying favorites little by little. If chicken with salsa is popular, how about white fish with salsa? Add mangoes one week if they are in season and pineapple the next. **Be creative when you branch out.**

FUN Hand all your family members a cookbook or the latest issue of *Cooking Light*. **Ask them to pick out one healthy-sounding recipe.** It'll be hard if they all choose dessert, but making them feel as though they're a part of the process is essential to the project's success.

FITNESS Encourage regular exercise. **Lead by example.** If you've got a family of couch potatoes, tell them dinner will be served after they run around the block.

FOCUS Be firm in your decisions to make positive, healthy changes. You are worth it. **You deserve this.** Your family will benefit greatly.

Homework Assignment Make a list of all your fears with regard to changing the way your family eats. Don't edit yourself, don't "hear" your spouse's complaints or your children's rants. Write freely. Next to each item, write down how your ideal self would approach the situation. Again, don't "hear" anyone's voice. This is your time to shine.

Feel your power and address these issues. The act of writing will help you get very clear about why you've been living this way up until now and how you will make the necessary changes. You may have to revisit this exercise a few times because it's just plain tough going up against the opposition.

YOUR GAME PLAN (STATE YOUR FOOD AND EXERCISE GOALS FOR THE WEEK)

Pasta with Sweet and Hot Peppers

SERVES 6 TO 8 *This recipe can be as hot as you want. You can light a match or burn down the house, depending on the peppers you choose.*

- 2 **tablespoons olive oil**
- 1 **medium onion, coarsely chopped**
- 2 **pounds mixed sweet and hot peppers, such as bell peppers and hot Italian peppers, seeded and cut into 1/4-inch-thick slices**
- 1 **garlic clove, minced**
  Coarse salt and cracked black pepper
- 1 **pound penne**
- 3/4 **cup chicken broth**
- 2 **tablespoons chopped fresh basil**

IN a large pot, bring salted water to a boil.

MEANWHILE, in a large skillet over medium heat, heat oil. Add onion, peppers, garlic, salt and pepper, cover, and cook for 15 to 20 minutes, stirring occasionally. Remove lid and add chicken broth and cook over high heat for 5 minutes, until sauce has reduced and thickened.

ADD penne to boiling water and cook following directions on package. When pasta is al dente, drain and return to pot, then immediately pour in sauce. Add basil, stir to combine, and serve.

■ *Bell peppers are the sweetest of the pepper family, so use more of them to cut down the heat. I like the red, yellow, and orange varieties. To turn up the heat, use banana peppers or hot Italian peppers.*

ZERO CALORIES, ZERO BARGAIN

Diet sodas may contain 0 sugar, 0 calories, and 0 fat, but they're no health bargain. The phosphate in diet soda may interfere with your body's ability to utilize calcium. Aspartame has been associated with birth defects, diabetes, seizures, and even brain tumors. Caffeine has been associated with insomnia, high blood pressure, irregular heartbeat, vitamin and mineral depletion, and more. To kick your soda or any habit that isn't serving you, post a goal for tomorrow: I will drink two bottles of water by suppertime tomorrow. I will drink one less diet soda. Think baby steps.

Monday

What I ate:

What I wish I hadn't:

What I did for exercise:

Tuesday

What I ate:

What I wish I hadn't:

What I did for exercise:

Wednesday

What I ate:

What I wish I hadn't:

What I did for exercise:

Thursday

What I ate:

What I wish I hadn't:

What I did for exercise:

Friday

What I ate:

What I wish I hadn't:

What I did for exercise:

REPORT CARD

I REALLY FELT GREAT WHEN I

I CAN GET BETTER AT

NEW FOODS I'M GOING TO TRY

NEXT WEEK I'M GOING TO

GIVE YOURSELF A GRADE
FOR THIS WEEK'S EFFORTS:

Saturday

What I ate:

What I wish I hadn't:

What I did for exercise:

Sunday

What I ate:

What I wish I hadn't:

What I did for exercise:

People ask me all the time if I think there's room for alcohol in a healthy diet, usually when I'm glued to the bar with an enormous Cosmopolitan in my hand. Whether you drink is a decision you need to make with your doctor. Research shows that moderate drinking (one to two glasses of wine a day) can benefit your heart and reduce the risks of stroke and diabetes in both men and women. Treat alcohol calories the same way you treat dessert calories—plan for them and earn them by cutting out something else and or by exercising accordingly.

kd@chefkathleen.com

SUBJECT: WINE FRIGHT
FROM: Hana
TO: kd@chefkathleen.com

Dear Kathleen,
My doctor is encouraging me to drink one glass of red wine a day. What kind of wine would you recommend?
  Hana

REPLY: FEAR NOT, WINE MAIDEN

Dear Hana,
The only time I drink wine is when I'm with chefs, wine connoisseurs, or my friend Maureen Christian Petrosky, author of *The Wine Club*. I rang her up and asked her if she'd give us both a crash course in nice reds to drink. Here's what she had to say: "If you like big-boy wines, wines with guts that go great with steak, stick to Cabernet Sauvignon and Zinfandel. If you're looking for something with lots of fruit, stay in California. But if it's an earthy, more complex sip you crave, stick to Old World reds, like those from France, Italy, and Spain. For one of my own faves, go Down Under for a spicy Shiraz."
  Kathleen

FOOD **A mini recipe:** For a fabulous hot-night or easy-entertaining dress-up dessert, Petrosky says, "Splash some champagne over a bowl of berries, toss with a sprinkling of sugar, and top with a dollop of fresh whipped cream." Send your kids to bed early and serve it in champagne glasses. Share with your sweetie.

FUN Maureen's bored book club went grapes when she started serving wine at their weekly gatherings. Learning about wine and food became their focus. **You don't need a fancy vocabulary or frenched-up cuisine to throw together a wine club of your own.** Invite over a bunch of your best girlfriends, get a group of singles together, or just grab the closest neighbors and explore the book already!

FITNESS Every single time I'm in a stressed-out funk, the first thing I want to do is ditch my workout and call an impromptu girls' night that may or may not include cocktails and "bad" food. I've learned that sometimes I need to get support and create accountability by telling someone I trust that I don't feel like working out. **I purposely call someone who will *not* tell me it's OK.** Working out reminds me of my inner strength, my ability to focus, and that I can choose to change my circumstances. The power is mine. Girls' night should be reserved as a time to nurture friendships, not as a time to enable unhealthy behavior.

FOCUS **Get into the habit of earning treat calories in advance of spending them.** Make a hard and fast rule that you can't spend them unless you've earned them. When there's no money left on your gift card, it's time to put down some more cash.

Homework Assignment Lock out denial. Retire anything that will aid and abet tendencies to stray and nest. Pack up your supping PJs, get rid of "those" comfort foods, ditch the sodas, dump the ice cream, toss the carryout menus. If nothing is around when you're looking to wine and dine yourself to destruction, you will find something else to do. Trust me. I know from experience.

YOUR GAME PLAN (STATE YOUR FOOD AND EXERCISE GOALS FOR THE WEEK)

Corn, Tomato, and Shrimp Salad

SERVES 4 *Here is a really refreshing summer (or anytime) salad. The colors of the salad will brighten up your day.*

- 4 **ears fresh corn**
- 1 **pound medium to large shrimp, shells on**
- 1 **pound ripe tomatoes, cored, cut into ½-inch chunks**
- ½–1 **jalapeño pepper, seeded and minced or grated**
- 2 **scallions, whites and greens, sliced thin**
- ¼ **loosely packed, coarsely chopped fresh basil**
- ¼ **cup fresh lemon juice**
- 2 **tablespoons white wine vinegar**
- 3 **tablespoons olive oil**
  Coarse salt and cracked black pepper to taste
- 4 **cups washed torn salad greens**

IN a medium pot of boiling salted water, boil corn for about 3 minutes. Remove corn with tongs. Let cool, then cut from cobs. Set aside.

PUT shrimp into boiling water and cook for about 2 minutes until pink. Drain water and let cool. Once cooled, peel shrimp and devein them.

PUT corn kernels, tomatoes, jalapeño, scallions, basil, and shrimp in a large bowl. Add lemon juice, vinegar, oil, salt, and pepper and toss to combine. Add the salad greens and toss to coat.

■ *Try serving with extra lemon for people like my dad who love to lay on the lemon.*

8 THINGS SUCCESSFUL DIETERS DO

According to the National Weight Control Registry, people who have maintained a 30-pound weight loss for five or more years have some things in common:

1. They eat breakfast.

2. They eat an average of five small meals a day.

3. They watch calories.

4. They eat high-carb, low-fat foods: 55 to 60 percent of their total daily calories come from fruits, vegetables, and other high-fiber foods.

5. They create accountability through journaling and weekly weigh-ins.

6. They get 60 to 90 minutes of exercise a day. Their number one choice? Good, old-fashioned walking.

7. They eat most of their meals at home.

8. They don't give up. Ever. Most failed more than once before they learned how to create healthy habits they could stick with for life.

What I ate:

What I wish I hadn't:

What I did for exercise:

Tuesday

What I ate:

What I wish I hadn't:

What I did for exercise:

Wednesday

What I ate:

What I wish I hadn't:

What I did for exercise:

Thursday

What I ate:

What I wish I hadn't:

What I did for exercise:

Friday

What I ate:

What I wish I hadn't:

What I did for exercise:

REPORT CARD

I REALLY FELT GREAT WHEN I

I CAN GET BETTER AT

NEW FOODS I'M GOING TO TRY

NEXT WEEK I'M GOING TO

GIVE YOURSELF A GRADE
FOR THIS WEEK'S EFFORTS:

Saturday

What I ate:

What I wish I hadn't:

What I did for exercise:

Sunday

What I ate:

What I wish I hadn't:

What I did for exercise:

Baby steps work. They're your only safe and sure hope, so you might as well take a deep breath and embrace the process. You can yo-yo some more if you haven't had enough of the I'm-skinny-no-I'm-fat-I'm-good-no-I'm-bad cycle. You can throw a few more bucks into the infomercial guy's pocket, buy a few dozen more diet books, or you can buckle down and move ahead.

SMALL IS BEAUTIFUL

Check out success-story Nancy's results from doing things little by little:

I'm living proof that small things done consistently do work! My triglycerides, once in the 300s, are now down to 127. And my cholesterol is 198. The first time it's ever been below 200. My HDL/LDL ratio is almost 3:1. My resting pulse rate is 55, down from 85 bpm.

If you're feeling like you're stuck and not "getting the job done," please stay with it. Get your blood work done on a regular basis. Many insurance companies pay for such testing at least once a year. It tells a lot about your inner health and can really keep you going when the scale isn't budging. I was a walking stroke–heart attack waiting to happen. Change, made slowly and in small steps, really did it for me.

FOOD When was the last time you had a bowl of lentils, a roasted beet, a serving of squash, some sautéed Swiss chard? **Work in some of the harder-to-work-in foods this week.** If you can cook spinach, you can cook Swiss chard. Wash chard, but do not spin or towel-dry. Using a paring knife, remove chard stems and slice as you would celery. Roughly chop the leaves into baby-spinach-size pieces. Place 2 teaspoons olive oil in a skillet over medium heat. Add minced garlic, a few capers, and a minced anchovy if you're a fan. Add the chard stems and cook a minute or so. Add the leaves and cook until fork-tender and wilted, about 2 to 3 minutes more. Turn off heat, squeeze the juice of half a lemon over chard, and toss once more. Serve immediately.

FUN Splurge on some decadent culinary provisions this week: a little block of Stilton cheese, expensive pears, a bottle of aged balsamic vinegar. **Staying inspired to cook is as important to your good health as exercise, rest, and play.**

FITNESS **During every workout this week, take a baby step forward, especially if you're "stuck."** Day 1: Walk five extra minutes. Day 2: Increase your walk pace to the fastest you can manage for one to five minutes. Day 3: Do a light jog or intense power walk for five to ten minutes some time during your workout. Day 4: Walk for five minutes, power walk, or jog for five minutes. Repeat this throughout your workout as often as you can. Day 5: Walk for ten extra minutes.

FOCUS **You cannot fail unless you quit.**

Homework Assignment In each category—food, fun, focus, and fitness—write down the next three baby steps you'd like to take. For instance, under "food" you might write:

I'm not eating beans very often. I will buy (or cook) beans this week.

I'm not getting enough servings of vegetables daily. I'll throw some cauliflower in the microwave while I take a shower, toss it with some lemon juice, olive oil, salt, pepper, and dried oregano, and throw it in the fridge for later.

I'm sneaking way too many Girl Scout cookies. I'm going to toss them. Next year, I'll write the girls a check and be done with it.

Stick to baby steps. There are no extremes among these examples. It doesn't help to say "I'll eat beans every day, I'll eat four servings of veggies every day, I'll never eat cookies again."

YOUR GAME PLAN (STATE YOUR FOOD AND EXERCISE GOALS FOR THE WEEK)

Carrot Slaw

SERVES 4 *All I can say is "supersimple." If you need a salad for the ladies' luncheon or a quick salad for dinner, this one is for you.*

¼ **cup fresh lemon juice**

1–2 **tablespoons olive oil**

1 **teaspoon sugar**

Coarse salt and cracked black pepper to taste

3 **cups shredded carrots (a 10-ounce bag)**

1–2 **tablespoons minced fresh parsley**

COMBINE all ingredients in a medium bowl, toss together, and serve.

EMPTY CALORIES

Before I put anything in my mouth or my shopping cart, I ask (myself) the same question: What's this going to buy me? It's easier to answer the question correctly (nothing) and do the right thing (abstain) if you have the conversation at the point of purchase rather than after. The question usually pops into my head only when I've got a bag of blue corn tortilla chips or something equally void of nutrition in my hand and I'm trying to justify it because they're baked with "whole-grain goodness," because chocolate's good for me, or because ice cream contains bone-strengthening calcium. Empty-calorie foods buy short-lived enjoyment and deprive you of more nutritious calories. The price? More time exercising and calorie cutbacks somewhere else.

Monday

What I ate:

What I wish I hadn't:

What I did for exercise:

Tuesday

What I ate:

What I wish I hadn't:

What I did for exercise:

Wednesday

What I ate:

What I wish I hadn't:

What I did for exercise:

Thursday

What I ate:

What I wish I hadn't:

What I did for exercise:

Friday

What I ate:

What I wish I hadn't:

What I did for exercise:

Saturday

I REALLY FELT GREAT WHEN I

I CAN GET BETTER AT

NEW FOODS I'M GOING TO TRY

NEXT WEEK I'M GOING TO

GIVE YOURSELF A GRADE
FOR THIS WEEK'S EFFORTS:

What I ate:

What I wish I hadn't:

What I did for exercise:

Sunday

What I ate:

What I wish I hadn't:

What I did for exercise:

WEEK 49
The Mix-and-Match Diet

I mixed and matched my way to a 75-pound weight loss, and if I can do it, so can you. Mix and match lazy work-outs with intense workouts. Mix and match splurges with extremely clean and healthy meals. Live like a boot camp detainee if you want to, but it's not necessary.

kd@chefkathleen.com

SUBJECT: WORK, WORK, WORK

FROM: Patricia
TO: kd@chefkathleen.com

Dear Kathleen,
I just can't seem to get myself started on a weight-loss program. I teach high school, am married, and don't have kids. We eat out frequently at night. I eat junk at school or go out with other teachers, and we usually say we're going to order healthy but don't. My breakfast is a scone or a muffin in the car on the way to school. I have so much to do for school that I don't have time to exercise. My doctor would like to see me lose 85 pounds. I feel overwhelmed.
Patricia

REPLY: WORK, WORK OUT, PLAY

Dear Patricia,
Don't think about 85 pounds, think 1 pound. Look into walking clubs or, better, start one with other teachers. Clean up your breakfast: oatmeal or whole-grain cereals with fresh fruit or a whole-grain English muffin with peanut butter and all-fruit jam, but no scones! They can easily contain 750 calories, and they don't fill you up. We had a group of teachers on the show who used to cook once a week. They cook at home and bring in lunch for everybody. They'd throw money in a pot, and each week it was someone's responsibility to bring in fresh fruit for snacks.

When you're super-stressed-out, rest, proper nutrition, and exercise are the keys to a greater ability to cope, productivity, and feelings of well-being. You don't let your students give up on themselves. Don't give up on yourself.
Kathleen

FOOD Wigging out? Instead of baking yourself back together again, do a kitchen workout to get rid of some of that nervous tension. **Open your fruit and veggie drawers and drag everything out.** Prep every vegetable and piece of fruit in the house. Cook up that squash taking up counter space. Cut up a melon. Surround yourself with low-calorie, beautifully prepared, and attractively presented wholesome foods. If your crisper compartment is empty, surely you have some brown rice and dried beans that you can cook and figure out what to do with later. Get busy. It's cheap, healthy, result-orientated, productive fun.

FUN **Schedule a nap for the middle of the afternoon.** And take it.

FITNESS Dr. Pamela Peeke, a fitness expert and author, says even five minutes of exercise can level out our stress hormones and will ease or eliminate "false" hunger pains. **I've found that sometimes five minutes of gardening or a quick walk to the mailbox works.** Sometimes I'm still hungry, but the time spent doing something else is time I can be rational and talk myself out of having three bowls of cereal in a row.

FOCUS **Taking control feels better than a belly full of anything.**

Homework Assignment Make your won't-give-up, can't-give-up to-morrow game plan. What can you do for exercise tomorrow? What could get in your way? What are you willing to do to compensate? Taking into consideration what you already have in the house to eat and what you will *realistically* do, what can you eat for a healthy breakfast, lunch, and dinner? What kind of healthy snacks can you plan for tomorrow? What are you willing to do to ensure that you won't give up? Do you want to live with a quitter's crown? I didn't think so.

YOUR GAME PLAN (STATE YOUR FOOD AND EXERCISE GOALS FOR THE WEEK)

Tomato, Spinach, and Tortellini Soup

SERVES 2 TO 3 *My mother loves this soup—partly because the mess is contained to one pot, one cutting board, and one knife. But also because it is delicious.*

1 **tablespoon olive oil**
1 **garlic clove, minced**
4 **cups chicken broth**
1 **14-ounce can diced tomatoes with liquid**
6 **ounces cheese tortellini**
1 **10-ounce bag prewashed baby spinach**
¼ **cup coarsely chopped, loosely packed basil**

HEAT oil in a medium saucepan over medium heat, add garlic, and cook until fragrant but not browned, 2 to 3 minutes. Add chicken broth and tomatoes and bring to a boil.

ADD tortellini and cook according to directions on package. Stir in spinach until wilted, 1 to 2 minutes. Serve sprinkled with basil.

GOOD FOR POPEYE AND GOOD FOR YOU!

Who knew spinach was a source of protein? Two grams per 1½-cup serving doesn't make it high-protein, but it's one more reason to feast on the tasty green. Spinach is an excellent source of vitamin A, vitamin C, and potassium. A 1½-cup serving also delivers a nice dose of dietary fiber, about 5 grams, and only 40 calories. A nutritional bargain for sure.

4 Ways to Work More Spinach into Your Diet

1. Use it as a base for salads.

2. Toss it into soups just before serving.

3. Add it to omelets and frittatas.

4. Google spinach recipes and print out ones you like.

Monday

What I ate:

What I wish I hadn't:

What I did for exercise:

Tuesday

What I ate:

What I wish I hadn't:

What I did for exercise:

Wednesday

What I ate:

What I wish I hadn't:

What I did for exercise:

Thursday

What I ate:

What I wish I hadn't:

What I did for exercise:

Friday

What I ate:

What I wish I hadn't:

What I did for exercise:

Saturday

I REALLY FELT GREAT WHEN I

I CAN GET BETTER AT

NEW FOODS I'M GOING TO TRY

NEXT WEEK I'M GOING TO

GIVE YOURSELF A GRADE
FOR THIS WEEK'S EFFORTS:

What I ate:

What I wish I hadn't:

What I did for exercise:

Sunday

What I ate:

What I wish I hadn't:

What I did for exercise:

Are Your Fears Making You Fat?

Focus on what you *can* do. Start by changing your outlook. Worry, fear, guilt, anger, and blame don't facilitate positive change. Do whatever it is you need to do to get in touch with your loving heart (the part that grows three sizes at the sound of a child's laughter), and start thinking about all the resources you have access to and make plans to utilize them. Nothing feels as good as closing the door on something that's taking up way too much of your time and energy.

kd@chefkathleen.com

SUBJECT: DIA-WHAT?
FROM: Angela
TO: kd@chefkathleen.com

Dear Kathleen,
I am 52 years old, 5 feet 3 inches,
and 250 pounds. I've been recently
diagnosed with type 2 diabetes. I've
been overweight most of my life.
I don't know what to do or eat.
   Angela

REPLY: CLICK ON DIABETES.ORG

Dear Angela,
Go to the American Diabetes Association's Web site, diabetes.org, or call 1-800-DIABETES for more information. The site is loaded! An appointment with a nutritionist who specializes in diabetes education can be an extremely worthwhile investment. The nurses in your doctor's office or your local chapter of the American Diabetes Association will be able to help you find someone. If money is an issue, keep in mind that there is nothing more important to spend your money on than your health. If you can afford only one appointment, phone the professional in advance and tell her that. There is no diet right for everyone, Angela. Through trial and error, you will create an eating and exercise program that works for you.
   Best wishes,
   Kathleen

FOOD **By taking the frying pan into his own hands and remaking his favorite dishes, Darly Heard took off 50 pounds!** To prepare his famous spicy Mexican-style burritos, add low-sodium taco seasoning to nonstick pan-"fried" ground white-meat chicken and cook until done. Toss some Spanish-rice seasoning mix into a batch of brown rice and put a scoop of each on warm whole-wheat tortillas spread with a thin layer of low-sodium refried beans. Top the whole thing with a sprinkling of a low-fat Mexican cheese like queso fresco (or low-fat Monterey Jack), a spoonful of salsa, and a dollop of Greek-style yogurt. Way to go!

FUN **Renew your library card and spend the whole afternoon rediscovering why libraries are so neat.**

FITNESS If you're procrastinating about weight training, find a nice clean spot on the floor, preferably on a carpeted floor, and do five girlie pushups from the knee. I don't care if you have to take fifteen-minute breaks between each one. Do five. **How do you feel?** Take the rest of the day off and repeat tomorrow. In the meantime, search the Web for some at-home weight-training DVDs if you have no interest in joining a gym.

FOCUS **Procrastinate on procrastinating.**

Homework Assignment You can't afford to backslide every time something comes up. Turning *to* food and *away* from exercise will only deepen your funk. Create new coping mechanisms, and practice using them when times aren't so tough. *I decided long ago that I was no longer willing to cope with life's curve balls while fat.* I just don't have enough energy to deal with problems and self-loathing. So I reach out for support. I turn to close friends, I go to counseling and read self-help books. Healing with a strong, healthy body makes a difference in how you feel and how you cope. Accessing support and eating right is free personal power. Figure out what's eating *you* and get the help you need. You deserve to be free from emotional strain and pain.

YOUR GAME PLAN (STATE YOUR FOOD AND EXERCISE GOALS FOR THE WEEK)

Celery and Blue Cheese Salad

SERVES 4 *This is a great make-ahead dish. You can toss all the ingredients into a storage container, put on the lid, shake, and store.*

8 **celery stalks, sliced very thin**
4 **ounces blue cheese, crumbled**
1 **tablespoon olive oil**
1–2 **tablespoons rice wine vinegar**
　Coarse salt and cracked black pepper to taste

COMBINE all ingredients in a medium bowl and toss together gently. Serve well chilled.

BLUE VELVET

Maytag Blue cheese was originally made by the guy who brought us the appliances of the same name. Fritz Maytag, the founder of the washing-machine company, was a cheese lover at heart. He started dabbling in cheese-making with scientists at Iowa State University near his home. To this day, Maytag is considered one of the greatest blue cheeses in the world, rivaling the very best Europe has to offer. The delicate creamy cheese is still hand-made after the original 1941 formula, and it's widely available in supermarkets and relatively inexpensive.

2 Ways to Have Your Blue Cheese and Still Fit into Your Blue Jeans

1. Split a blue cheese burger with a friend.

2. Make your own blue-cheese dressing: whisk together ¼ cup crumbled blue cheese with ¼ cup low-fat buttermilk, ¼ cup nonfat Greek-style yogurt, and 2 teaspoons white vinegar. Season to taste with salt and pepper.

Monday

What I ate:

What I wish I hadn't:

What I did for exercise:

Tuesday

What I ate:

What I wish I hadn't:

What I did for exercise:

Wednesday

What I ate:

What I wish I hadn't:

What I did for exercise:

Thursday

What I ate:

What I wish I hadn't:

What I did for exercise:

Friday

What I ate:

What I wish I hadn't:

What I did for exercise:

REPORT CARD

I REALLY FELT GREAT WHEN I

I CAN GET BETTER AT

NEW FOODS I'M GOING TO TRY

NEXT WEEK I'M GOING TO

GIVE YOURSELF A GRADE
FOR THIS WEEK'S EFFORTS:

Saturday

What I ate:

What I wish I hadn't:

What I did for exercise:

Sunday

What I ate:

What I wish I hadn't:

What I did for exercise:

WEEK 51
When Your Paunch Runneth Over

New girth doesn't sprout overnight. Keeping weight off requires the same good habits that taking weight off requires. You might be able to afford a few more calories when you're maintaining, but the same temptations greet you a hundred times a day. Losing weight and keeping it off means planning ahead and thinking on your feet. Wrenching yourself from the grips of self-sabotage and the jaws of jelly-filled donuts is manageable and doable.

kd@chefkathleen.com

SUBJECT: WHEN YOUR FAT JEANS ARE TIGHT
FROM: Shelby
TO: kd@chefkathleen.com

Dear Kathleen,
When you're up a few pounds, what do you do?
    Shelby

REPLY: FIGHT BACK!

Dear Shelby,
I set the oven timer for 15 minutes, throw a good fit, and play the blame game. "It's not my fault, I'm getting older. The dry cleaner shrinks *everything*. I'm retaining water." When the timer goes off, the pity party is over and it's time to take action.

First I identify what it is I've been eating too much of. Next, I fortify the barracks. I get rid of all the junk even if it's healthy junk. In times of extreme stress, I don't even keep cereal in the house. It's old-fashioned oatmeal or nothing. I cook like there's a prize for the greatest number of prepared healthy dishes stuffed into a refrigerator. I steam all my veggies, cook off a batch of brown rice, cut up every last piece of fruit, organize my freezer meals, and make plans to cook more if I'm low. And, finally, I hightail it to the gym for a vigorous purge-the-paunch workout.
    Kathleen

FOOD Whittle off a pound. Cut out salty foods, empty-calorie processed foods, and chunky portions this week. **Work in an extra salad meal.** Toss a bag of washed baby spinach leaves with lots of strawberry slices, some dried cranberries or clementine sections, a sprinkling of toasted sesame seeds, a drizzle of balsamic vinegar, and a splash of extra-virgin olive oil. Season to taste with salt and pepper.

FUN **Plan a potluck.** Ask everyone to bring something new and healthy along with printed copies of the recipe.

FITNESS Cardio is the best revenge. **There's nothing like a few endorphins to kick a good depression in the aaasssparagus.**

FOCUS Nothing is fun when you're obsessing about your weight. Do you want to keep your funk alive or enjoy the happiness you deserve? Choose life! **Practice being happy and thankful, no matter what your size.** It will come naturally after a while. I promise. Repeat after me: I am not my weight! Do not allow yourself to cop out, give in, or give up. Stay the course. Fight the fight.

Homework Assignment When you're feeling positive and in control, make a list of healthy (grown and packaged by Mother Nature) foods you really enjoy. Compare the list to what you have in the house. Aha! Stock up now.

YOUR GAME PLAN (STATE YOUR FOOD AND EXERCISE GOALS FOR THE WEEK)

Strawberry Rhubarb Sauce

SERVES 6 *This dessert is lovely and light by itself or on top of some Guilt-Free Vanilla Gelato (Week 31). My sister likes to top toast with it in the morning, and Dad mixes it into his oatmeal. You can refrigerate it for up to 2 weeks.*

1 **pound rhubarb, cut into 1-inch pieces**

¼–½ **cup sugar (to taste)**

1 **quart fresh strawberries, cleaned and sliced**

IN an 8-cup microwavable bowl, place rhubarb, sugar, and 2 tablespoons water.

COOK on high, uncovered, for 5 minutes and then for 1-minute intervals until you have a saucelike consistency. Remove from microwave, immediately add strawberries, and stir. The heat from the rhubarb will cook the strawberries just the right amount.

COOL to room temperature and serve or store in refrigerator for later use.

SLEEP BUSTERS

Caffeine and/or alcohol consumed within four to six hours of bedtime can affect your ability to get a good night's sleep. Skip the afternoon latte, and if alcohol is on the menu, drink early (it's 5:00 P.M. *somewhere*), drink plenty of water, and limit your intake.

Scientific studies show mounting correlations between lack of sleep and disease. According to the National Sleep Foundation, getting too little sleep can increase the secretion of a growth hormone linked to obesity. Since blood pressure usually falls during the sleep cycle, interrupting shuteye can lead to hypertension and cardiovascular problems. Research has also shown that insufficient sleep impairs the body's ability to use insulin, which can lead to the onset of diabetes.

What I ate:

What I wish I hadn't:

What I did for exercise:

Tuesday

What I ate:

What I wish I hadn't:

What I did for exercise:

Wednesday

What I ate:

What I wish I hadn't:

What I did for exercise:

Thursday

What I ate:

What I wish I hadn't:

What I did for exercise:

Friday

What I ate:

What I wish I hadn't:

What I did for exercise:

REPORT CARD

I REALLY FELT GREAT WHEN I

I CAN GET BETTER AT

NEW FOODS I'M GOING TO TRY

NEXT WEEK I'M GOING TO

GIVE YOURSELF A GRADE
FOR THIS WEEK'S EFFORTS:

Saturday

What I ate:

What I wish I hadn't:

What I did for exercise:

Sunday

What I ate:

What I wish I hadn't:

What I did for exercise:

WEEK
51

The Baby-Step Miracle Diet

Never give up on yourself, never stop trying. When you feel hopeless, take a baby step out of the pain, and then another, until help and hurt turn back into hope. When you have hope, you will achieve success. Seek out the resources available to you: your families and friends, your doctors, your community services, your clergy, your peers, and mostly yourself. If I can get up and do this every day, you can too! My very best wishes for great health!

READ THIS EVERY TIME YOU FEEL DOWN

From real-life success story Roberta Brecher, the first guest I ever had on my show, *Cooking Thin:*

I was at my lowest point ever in my lifelong struggle to lose weight, having ballooned up to a ghastly 293 pounds. I had little hope for ever living life normally.

A couple of years have passed since that day. I've lost 137 pounds. Now I can shop in regular-size departments, and I don't have to settle for whatever fits anymore. I have discovered new passions for swimming and cooking fabulous, healthy meals. I have learned the magic of portion control and have not eaten one single frozen TV dinner in a very long time. I've learned the pleasure of just one cookie and how to trade a little extra exercise for the occasional treat. I can say this from the bottom of my heart with tremendous conviction: If I can do this, anyone can! I did it one step at a time.

FOOD Mother Nature provides for our nutritional needs abundantly. Stick to her bounty.

FUN Laughter is the best medicine, and it's good for your heart. A University of Maryland study revealed that laughter appears to expand the tissue that forms the inner lining of blood vessels, increasing blood flow. Dr. Michael Miller, director of Preventive Cardiology at the University of Maryland Medical Center, says, "We recommend that you try to laugh on a regular basis. **Thirty minutes of exercise, three times a week, and fifteen minutes of laughter a day is good for the vascular system.**" Create joy and laughter in your life.

FITNESS You don't have to like it **You just have to do it.**

FOCUS You can achieve positively everything you set your mind to.

Homework Assignment School's *out*! There's no homework.

Chocolate Fondue Party

SERVES 10 TO 12 *Most recipes for chocolate fondue call for a cup of heavy whipping cream, which makes for a nice, creamy fondue that clings gloriously to the items you're dipping — but 821 calories and 88 grams of fat in the whipping cream is a high price to pay.*

As the chocolate in this recipe cools, you may have to zap it in 10-second intervals on high in the microwave. So be sure the serving dish you choose is microwave-proof.

Deciding what to dip depends entirely upon the crowd you're serving. I strive for a superhealthy spread polka-dotted with a few no-no's, such as small cookies or fancy pretzels. Portion-control this dessert by putting out only one or two over-the-top-decadent treats per guest.

12 ounces bittersweet or semi-sweet chocolate chips or small bits

Assorted fresh fruit for dipping: strawberries; sliced apricots, peaches, pears, nectarines, kiwis; cherries with their stems; pineapple chunks; star fruit

Assorted dried fruits and nuts, for dipping: dried apricots, pineapple, and pears; whole pecans, walnuts, and cashews

Assorted "no-no's": miniature biscotti, shortbread, or other small cookies

WARM chocolate chips in a heavy small saucepan over lowest possible heat for 12 to 18 minutes, or until completely melted. To microwave, place 1 cup chocolate chips in an uncovered microwave-safe bowl on high for 1 minute; stir. Return to microwave and cook in 10- to 20-second intervals, stirring until smooth. To melt 2 cups, microwave for a few seconds longer.

PLACE bowl of chocolate in the center of a large platter of dippables. Serve immediately with small skewers or fancy toothpicks.

Learning to right yourself and rebound from setbacks is part of the game. Join me live and "in person" at chefkathleen. com. It's a free online re source designed to keep you entertained and on track. It's a source of motivation, support, and accountability.

On the forums, we trade "Help! I ate a bag of chips" disasters, recipes, and tips galore. There are daily home work assignments, success stories, book reviews, newsy bits of health information, and food facts galore. I'm there every single day answering questions and posting new information. We have a lot of fun. You don't have to use your real name when you register or even give a "real" e-mail address. Protecting your privacy is paramount to me. The site is a place for you to retreat in the privacy of your own home. Log on!

Monday

What I ate:

What I wish I hadn't:

What I did for exercise:

Tuesday

What I ate:

What I wish I hadn't:

What I did for exercise:

Wednesday

What I ate:

What I wish I hadn't:

What I did for exercise:

Thursday

What I ate:

What I wish I hadn't:

What I did for exercise:

Friday

What I ate:

What I wish I hadn't:

What I did for exercise:

Saturday

I REALLY FELT GREAT WHEN I

What I ate:

What I wish I hadn't:

I CAN GET BETTER AT

What I did for exercise:

Sunday

NEW FOODS I'M GOING TO TRY

What I ate:

What I wish I hadn't:

NEXT WEEK I'M GOING TO

What I did for exercise:

GIVE YOURSELF A GRADE
FOR THIS WEEK'S EFFORTS: